Elmore Leonard

Twayne's United States Authors Series

Frank Day, Editor

Clemson University

TUSAS 713

ELMORE LEONARD.
Courtesy of Elmore Leonard.

Elmore Leonard

James E. Devlin

State University of New York College at Oneonta

Twayne Publishers
New York

Twayne's United States Authors Series No. 713

Elmore Leonard
James E. Devlin

Twayne Publishers
1633 Broadway
New York, NY 10019

Library of Congress Cataloging-in-Publication Data

Devlin, James E., 1938 –
    Elmore Leonard / James E. Devlin.
        p.   cm. — (Twayne's United States authors series ; TUSAS 713)
    Includes bibliographical references and index.
    ISBN 0-8057-1694-7 (alk. paper)
    1. Leonard, Elmore, 1925 –   —Criticism and interpretation.
    2. Detective and mystery stories, American—History and criticism.
    I. Title.   II. Series.
    PS3562.E55Z64   1999
    813'.54—dc21   99-42756
                                                                              CIP

This paper meets the requirements of ANSI/NISO Z3948-1992 (Permanence of Paper).

10 9 8 7 6 5 4 3 2 1

Printed in the United States of America

To my people from Boston, Breslau, Brooklyn—and the Maineiacs!

Contents

Preface

By the late nineties, it had become impossible to ignore Elmore Leonard, whose ubiquitous presence on best-seller lists and on movie screens greeted readers and moviegoers at every turn. Dutch Leonard has been writing for a half century, in that time producing 35 novels (in addition to short stories and screenplays) and achieving a readership most authors only dream of. The 1995 Christmas season saw the film success *Get Shorty*, featuring some of Hollywood's top stars. In early 1998, *Rum Punch* came to the screen as Quentin Tarantino's *Jackie Brown;* some weeks later, *Cuba Libre* hit the *New York Times* best-seller list for four or five weeks, and *Out of Sight* ran through the summer in movie theaters across the country. These events produced a flurry of newspaper and magazine articles reminding Americans of how long Leonard has been writing "crime fiction," the genre that has nearly replaced what was once called "the mystery story."

Although he adamantly denies the influence of Philip Marlowe, Raymond Chandler, Dashiell Hammett, and James M. Cain, claiming, "I've never done a private eye," most readers will discern in Leonard's streets and alleys the shadows of earlier sleuths (as well as Mickey Spillane's Mike Hammer) and recognize that his noir settings—Miami Beach or Detroit—share elements with these practitioners of the detective story. Furthermore, his main characters bear marked resemblance to Hemingway's code heroes (highly responsible men who live by self-imposed rules). Like Hemingway, whom Leonard studied in the fifties and invariably credits as an influence, he writes about alienated, divorced, rootless men, sometimes lapsed in their Catholicism but still morally responsible, courageous, and as true to themselves as they are to their friends, for loyalty is one of the most admired virtues in the Leonard panoply.

Once Leonard discovered in the early fifties that he wanted to be a writer—rather than the copywriter he was—he set his sights on Western stories, not just because he recognized that he "wasn't going to be a literary writer," but because he liked this kind of fiction, in demand in both the pulps and the glossies. Although he knew little of the West himself, he had enjoyed the classic Hollywood oaters of the thirties and forties. In fact, American pop culture—above all, the movies—is comfortably at home in, even a hallmark of, Leonard's work.

His success at Westerns was not instantaneous, but in 1961 the Western Writers of America chose *Hombre* (1961) "as one of the twenty-five best western novels of all time," and the book was later made into a rousing Paul Newman movie. But Leonard was not satisfied with five Western novels and two dozen short stories, though even today he insists that his next career move came only when the Western print market vanished as television triumphed in the late fifties.

Although he did not abandon the Western in one swoop, he began a shift toward the crime novels that would establish his reputation. This transition from Western story to crime fiction represents an artistic progress he has continued as his reputation has grown. *Elmore Leonard* is itself evidence that Leonard's writing has achieved acknowledgment for its literary value.

A reading of Leonard's work reveals that the Western years were the great trying ground for later and richer efforts. A certain woodenness vanishes; plots become looser; dialogue approaches the perfection that led one critic to call Leonard's ear "Panasonic"; exposition grows more indebted to individual scenes; and the comic, so much a part of his writing that it is difficult to believe it was not always there, becomes an identifying characteristic of his unique "sound."

Leonard modestly regards himself as a storyteller, but he has come to recognize that his specialty—violent crime—has long since left the corner of the library where escapists sought "mystery stories" to enter the mainstream of letters as a legitimate concern of the nation's most accomplished writers, and he has come to recognize his part in bringing about that change. Today, after pioneer efforts in studies of actual criminals by Truman Capote and Norman Mailer, novelists such as John Updike and Joyce Carol Oates, successful both critically and popularly, employ themes involving crime and violence; and dozens of talented contemporary figures including Raymond Carver, Richard Ford, and Andre Dubus—whose short fiction crowds college literature anthologies—explore criminal behavior. At the millennium, violent crime seems no longer remote and titillating but a compelling fact of everyday life.

Today Leonard is generally regarded as the first among equals by competitors ranging from Donald Westlake to Ed McBain and even Robert B. Parker. Pop writers such as Stephen King and Andrew Greeley salute him, and he is regularly reviewed by prominent literary figures such as the late Walker Percy, who asked in an essay on *Bandits*

(1987) more than a decade ago: "Why is Leonard so good?" only to con-
clude that he is "the greatest crime writer of our time."

To answer Percy's question and to show why he reached his jubilant
conclusion are the purposes of this book, for which Leonard has granted
me days of interviews and access to correspondence. In other words, I
shall be considering Leonard's dazzling style and original motifs, peering
into his dangerous world of compromises and hope with crossed fingers.
His violent stories are suspenseful and understated, written in an American plain style in which an inimitable dialogue alternates with brief
narrative passages, making use of the limited descriptive touches that a
quick and deft painter might achieve. For the faster setting of scenes
and looser and much racier dialogue of his later books, he modestly
credits George V. Higgins, whose small-time urban hoods have left their
mark on Leonard's own as they outline their impractical schemes for the
bonanza that will transform their aimless lives.

Leonard writes exclusively from a third-person perspective, confidently entering the minds of large numbers of characters but always
returning to one. His sense of place is as highly developed as that of the
best American regionalists of the last hundred years, even when he
retreats to earlier times or foreign settings—a knack he learned from the
Western, always a historical novel. In *The Moonshine War* (1969), for
example, he creates a credible Prohibition-era Kentucky.

In his lifetime, particularly since World War II, Leonard has witnessed profound changes: the country's population has doubled, its city
centers have imploded, and its racial and ethnic mixtures have shifted.
These changes are reflected in his characters, who are trained in no par-
ticular skills and whose lives are little touched by culture or tradition.
They live in eroded cities like Detroit or Miami, where jobs are hard to
find and pay minimum wages and where even the lower middle class has
begun to lose direction as Ford or General Motors lays off workers and
institutions like the church falter.

His villains, on the other hand, often reflect his generation's experience with fascism and the evil men of energy and power: manipulative,
deceitful, persuasive, and the most possessed adherents of their own narcissistic vision.

The documentation of everyday life that accompanies his narrative,
ranging from guns to gold or from films to funeral parlors, is nearly
flawless. He is never creakily out-of-date like such popular writers of the
past as J. P. Marquand or Erskine Caldwell. A Leonard novel, whether it

involves a car jacking or the Federal Witness Protection Program, succeeds in encapsulating its time.

Also in the American naturalistic tradition is Leonard's predilection
for the grotesque, perhaps the influence of Caldwell or of other southern
writers. Especially frequent are psychopaths like Skip Gibbs of *Freaky
Deaky* (1988) or Blackbird of *Killshot* (1980), whom Leonard sees every-
where in America. Merciless and cold-blooded killers, they are also
childlike in their eagerness to be distracted by novelty or "glitz." Their
groping noncomprehension of normal standards of behavior that others
respect makes them dangerous to the morally bankrupt who use their
services and ultimately leads to their defeat by those normal, decent folk
they mindlessly seek to destroy; for Elmore Leonard is a conventional
moralist, believing that crime—real, vicious crime—does not pay.

As a new century begins, Elmore "Dutch" Leonard is both a successful and a wealthy writer. He commands huge advances and receives million-dollar contracts for movie rights. For these reasons alone, he is
bound to arouse suspicion by those who forget that mass audiences,
Hollywood recognition, and generous remunerations have been the
reward of many distinguished American writers. Popularity and excel-
lence need not be mutually exclusive. Of great and genuine ability,
Leonard is both a stylist and a keen observer of changing America, a living author who deserves acknowledgment at this late stage in his pro-
ductive life.

Acknowledgments

Many have assisted me in the preparation of this volume, and I am truly grateful for their help.

First I should like to thank Elmore Leonard and his wife, Christine, who treated me with unfailing courtesy and kindness; then my wife Maria, critic and typist, whose *Sitzfleisch* will always exceed my own.

Thanks are due also to David Geherin, whose own graceful *Elmore Leonard* was of great assistance.

To the following librarians, I owe a debt of gratitude: Christine Yancy, McNichols Campus Library, University of Detroit; and at Milne Library, College at Oneonta: Mary Lou Benson, Christine Bulson, Andrea Gerber, Sally Goodwin, Elaine Downing, and others.

I wish also to thank my colleague Paul Jensen for sharing his movie lore with me, and Investigator Kenneth Sosnowski, Bureau of Criminal Investigation, New York State Police, for technical assistance.

Finally, I am grateful to the College at Oneonta for a Faculty Research Grant, the Walter B. Ford Grant, and a Professional Development Grant.

Chronology

1925   Elmore John Leonard born 11 October in New Orleans.

1943   Graduates from Detroit University High School and enters navy.

1946   Returns to Detroit and enrolls at the University of Detroit.

1949   Marries Beverly Cline.

1950   Graduates from college and begins work at Campbell-Ewald advertising agency in Detroit.

1951   Breaks into print with "Trail of the Apache" in *Argosy*.

1953   *The Bounty Hunters* published by Houghton Mifflin.

1957   First two movies based on Leonard's work appear, *3:10 to Yuma* and *The Tall T*.

1961   Leaves Campbell-Ewald, hoping to become a full-time writer, but freelances in advertising and works on educational films.

1965   Hollywood buys *Hombre;* Leonard returns to writing.

1966   H. N. Swanson, big-time Hollywood agent, takes Leonard as writing client and manuscript of *The Big Bounce*.

1967   *Hombre,* starring Paul Newman.

1969   *The Big Bounce* published, marking Leonard's break with Westerns; sells *The Broke-Leg War* (later *The Moonshine War*) to the movies; *The Big Bounce,* starring Ryan O'Neal.

1970   *Valdez Is Coming*.

1972   *Forty Lashes Less One;* movie of *The Moonshine War;* first screenplay, *Joe Kidd,* starring Clint Eastwood.

1974   *Mr. Majestyk,* starring Charles Bronson; *52 Pick-Up*.

1977   *Unknown Man # 89;* divorced from Beverly Cline.

1978   Spends weeks at Detroit Police Headquarters; *The Switch,* nominated for an Edgar by the Mystery Writers of America.

1979   Marries Joan Shepard.

1980   Donald Fine of Arbor House begins promoting Leonard; *Gold Coast,* first Florida setting; *City Primeval,* first cop protagonist.

1981   Starts association with Gregg Sutter, who becomes Leonard's research assistant.

1984   *LaBrava* wins an Edgar as best mystery novel of the year.

1985   *Glitz* hits the *New York Times* best-seller list; Leonard's picture on cover of *Newsweek; Stick,* starring Burt Reynolds.

1986   *52 Pick-Up,* starring Roy Scheider and Ann Margaret.

1987   *Bandits,* most political novel; *Touch,* written a decade earlier, least characteristic novel.

1990   *Get Shorty.*

1991   *Maximum Bob.*

1992   *Rum Punch.*

1993   Wife Joan dies of cancer; Leonard marries Christine Kent.

1995   *Get Shorty,* starring John Travolta, number one movie in America its first week; *Riding the Rap.*

1997   *Jackie Brown,* directed by Quentin Tarantino, based on *Rum Punch,* opens Christmas Day.

1998   *Out of Sight,* directed by Steven Soderbergh, called "best film" at year's end by National Society of Film Critics; *Cuba Libre.*

1999   *Be Cool;* Leonard appears in the Land's End catalog, endorsing Chili Palmer styles; Coca Cola inserts promotional samples of *Be Cool* in 12- and 24-packs of Diet Coke.

Chapter One
Biography

Calihan Hall

In the early afternoon of 10 May 1997, Elmore Leonard, a short, slender figure in his early seventies, crosses the stage at Calihan Hall to accept an honorary doctorate of humane letters from the University of Detroit. It is a blue spring day, perfect for a triumphant return to the campus he left almost 50 years earlier, a young navy veteran back from the Pacific.

Now, in borrowed academic garb and wearing a wispy gray beard the Jesuits would have frowned on, with more than 30 novels—not to mention short stories, TV productions, and films—behind him, Leonard looks out over the crowd. Still chiefly a pop writer, he is starting to attract serious critical interest. The college, he realizes, like the reviewers, has stopped hedging its bets.

But he is pleased to be back. Still a Catholic, at least a nominal one, he had chafed like so many of the faithful at certain strictures of the church, rejecting some but never all. He is grateful, he will be saying shortly, to his Jesuit teachers for pounding some Latin and Greek into his head, but even more for awakening a love of learning. The oppressive nature of Catholic education so many have chronicled is not in the portrait of this artist. Rather, America's monarch of crime fiction, a writer with a reputation built on depicting the seedy and marginal figures of the small-time underworld, takes a more characteristically cheerful view in real life. The priests, he feels, did all right by him.

Just a typical American boy interested in girls, movies, pop music, and sports, Leonard has been nicknamed "Dutch" by everyone since high school (and still is) after Dutch Leonard, a widely regarded knuckleballer for the Washington Senators with a respectable lifetime average of 191 wins, 113 losses—sort of baseball's equivalent of the solid B average Leonard earned in four years at the University of Detroit. But now practically everyone sitting out there knows him. Unlike his namesake, Dutch Leonard has gotten into the hall of fame. Most of the graduates have seen *Get Shorty* with John Travolta, Danny DeVito, and Gene

Hackman, and many have read Leonard's new novel *Out of Sight,* seven weeks on the *New York Times* best-seller list.

But even 10 or 12 years earlier, Leonard had been happy with the way things were going, up from the fifties when he had begun writing Western stories, mainly for the pulps. His first printed story, a 13,000-word novelette called "Trail of the Apache" (1951), had been accepted by the men's magazine *Argosy* for $1,000 and had brought a letter from a literary agent in New York saying: "You seem to have a real knowledge of these Indians' habits."[1]

In the mid- to late fifties, when the coaxial cable drove Westerns from movie screens and the pulps to TV, before the end of the decade, Dutch Leonard knew he'd have to switch his focus from stories set in the Arizona Territory to something else, a change he eventually made so well that by the early eighties his crime fiction was being called "the best the genre has to offer" by *Newsweek.*[2] And 1997? Well, it would be an annus mirabilis: five movies, not counting made-for-TVs.

His speech to the new graduates will be mercifully short. As a working writer, he feels most comfortable reading his pages aloud. On an occasion like this, he just improvises.

He begins with a tribute to the Jesuits, then introduces a Zulu proverb in deference to the many black faces (not to be seen in his student days), the standard graduation sort of thing about not waiting for the future but going out to meet it. But it is a genuine Bantu proverb—Leonard leaves nothing to chance—found the previous day as he was leafing through *Smithsonian.* The words reflect what he has done himself, and they fit the aspirations of the young people he is addressing.

Leonard's Place

Leonard's success has certainly not come overnight. He went through an apprenticeship of nearly two decades, suffering a severe setback in the early sixties when he published nothing for five years and radically changed the direction of his writing once. Today, however, he is the darling of the critics, many of whom are unaware that he began writing Westerns set in the late-nineteenth-century Arizona Territory.

As a pop writer, Leonard is both suspicious and flattered to find himself included in college literature courses and being invited to writing conferences. Like others before him—Erskine Caldwell comes to mind—Leonard tends to equate popularity with worth. If hundreds of thousands want him, he must be good. At the same time, he is deeply gratified by critical recognition, though he wonders what is being talked about when he spots a reviewer going on about the theme of "redemption" in his books. He grows almost as prickly when a French reader writes to say a dead bolt can't be blasted open with a shotgun rigged out with a special barrel attachment—"Tell the Detroit police," Leonard grumps. Told there is a voyeuristic quality to much of his fiction, in which breaking and entering plays a significant role, he smiles and says that that's what storytellers do: they look at other people and their things.

Measured by standards of both critical and popular success, Leonard is at the peak of his powers. The popularity of movies based on his work shows that he is capable not only of writing gripping thrillers with comic figures but of writing real comedy and trenchant satire. The cover of the German edition of *Get Shorty* notes that the novel is "at once a fast-paced thriller and a barbed satire of the American way of life." *Cuba Libre,* on the other hand, a novel of the Spanish-American War with allusions to characters and events from *Gunsights* (1979), served to remind reviewers that Leonard started by writing historical novels.

In the nineties, Leonard regularly receives notices such as Scott Bradfield's salute in the *Times Literary Supplement* apprising British readers of the "funniest hard-boiled writer America has to offer these days," and *Booklist* calls him a "modern master" in a review of *Out of Sight* in 1996 and alerts libraries to the fact that "nobody writes snappier dialogue" in considering *Riding the Rap* (1995).[3]

Life

Leonard's half-century writing career, leading to a point where crime fiction scholar David Geherin judges his books "among the finest crime novels ever written," worthy of "a permanent place beside those of Hammett and Chandler on the shelf marked simply Outstanding American Fiction," begins on 11 October 1925 in New Orleans.[4] Born to Elmore John Leonard and Flora Rivé Leonard, he received his father's Christian name when his mother gracefully deferred to an in-law's assumption that she would be naming the new baby after his father. The Leonards were Irish, and the mother's side, despite the Gallic-sounding name, originated in Alsace. Elmore Sr. had worked a variety of jobs, and when his son was born, he was employed by General Motors as part of a team locating new spots for GM dealerships, a mission that took the senior Leonard, his wife, Elmore Jr., and his older sister to zone offices in several states. In the years following 1927 or 1928, Dutch Leonard recalls moving to Dallas, to Oklahoma City, back to Dallas, to Detroit for six months, to Memphis for two and a half years, and finally permanently to Detroit. In 1947 the senior Leonard, whose fortunes had risen steadily from the jazz age, opened his own automobile dealership in Las Cruces, New Mexico. Here he hoped his son would join him selling cars unavailable during the war to hungry American buyers, but he died within six months of starting the agency. When Leonard—whose interest in cars was lukewarm—returned to Detroit, he found that the city was not interested in taking a chance with a novice.

Young as he had been in the New Orleans years (spent in a four-family flat on Carrollton Avenue), Louisiana left an indelible impression on Leonard, and New Orleans and its environs surface in books as unalike as *Bandits* and *Cuba Libre*. More telling yet are photos from his childhood days in Oklahoma City and Memphis showing young Elmore posed with toy revolvers—foreshadowing, perhaps, later concerns, though he claims never to have owned a real gun despite an aficionado's fondness for their depiction in his novels and a study full of old firearms catalogs and *Shooter's Bibles*. In one of these photos, taken at about age nine, Leonard poses, his left foot planted on the running board of what appears to be an Oakland sedan, wearing the sort of soft-visored cap he still favors—his interest in headgear being almost as consuming as his attention to guns—and aiming a revolver menacingly at the camera. This snapshot, he claims, is his version of the notorious photograph of Bonnie Parker that flooded newspapers and magazines about the time she met her maker with Clyde Barrow in a police ambush on 23 May 1934 near Sailes in Bienville Parish, Louisiana. Today Leonard shakes his head at the photo but insists that fancies from the years between ages 5 and 10 will often influence a life's work.

In Detroit, starting in 1934, Leonard was enrolled first at Blessed Sacrament, a parochial elementary school, and later at the University of Detroit High School, a Catholic prep school that sent many of its graduates on to the University of Detroit or to other Catholic colleges. At this time, before the war, Leonard was thinking of attending Georgetown and its School of Foreign Service, vaguely envisioning himself as a diplomat in some exotic corner of the world, an ambition largely inspired by the movies. At University of Detroit High School, he played first-string baseball and football on teams competing citywide in Class A, but he is reticent about his performance, admitting that his height and weight would certainly handicap him in today's Detroit. Although he was a bookish and imaginative schoolboy, nothing in those days foretells a literary career. To be sure, he tried his hand at a story or two like most kids. In the fifth grade, he recalls composing a play based on Erich Maria Remarque's *All Quiet on the Western Front* (1929), then being serialized in the newspaper. Among other dubious casting decisions, he gave his class's only black youth the role of a German soldier.

In 1943, the year he graduated from high school, Leonard attempted to enlist in the Marine Corps but was turned down for failing an eye test. Later that year he was drafted into the navy, where—after training in Rhode Island—he spent most of his hitch with the Seabees in New Guinea and the Admiralty Islands. His experience seems to have been less like John Wayne's (*The Fighting Seabees*, 1944) and more like that of the crew aboard the supply ship USS *Reluctant* (*Mr. Roberts*, 1955). Leonard did a variety of mundane jobs around the airstrip his construction battalion maintained for U.S. Navy and Commonwealth pilots, among them handing out the beer for which he developed a perhaps too enthusiastic taste. He saw plenty of movies supplied from stateside and came under fire only once, when the Japanese made a halfhearted bombing raid. Still, the navy opened his eyes. He enjoyed strutting about the Philippines and later California in the skintight blues that young sailors had specially tailored, cuffs rolled back the de rigeur couple of inches, and white cap rakishly tilted. He liked beer, movies, baseball, and the girls he met on the rare chances he had to visit the USO or a dance hall in the Philippines. Once, on the very day he had had his wallet lifted while showering, he decided to get a tattoo. Envisioning an elaborately nautical Seabees emblem, he found that the bill a buddy had lent him was a one and not a ten, and that one dollar would buy either "USN" or "Dutch" in two colors. "Dutch" is still there on his left shoulder, though the red has faded away.[5]

Released from the navy, Leonard returned home to find that the charms of an eastern campus at an older university had largely dissipated, and he abandoned ideas of Georgetown for the University of Detroit, a campus with many of its buildings only a score of years old, ready to receive the hordes of veterans the GI Bill was pushing into American colleges. While there he met and married Beverly Cline, his first wife, with whom he eventually had five children. When his father died, a year before Leonard finished college, he thought about taking over the family auto business in New Mexico with his sister Margaret's husband. The GM regional manager put the kibosh on that idea—for which Leonard is eternally grateful—suggesting that the young man look into advertising, a growing field that Leonard agreed seemed more appealing than peddling cars, though he was somewhat vague about what "advertising" entailed. Sent to the Campbell-Ewald advertising agency in Detroit with the briefest sort of introduction, Leonard landed a job after graduation, one roughly as important as the one he had held in the navy—"their first married office boy," he likes to say.

Advertising

The young husband and father stayed on his first tour of duty with Campbell-Ewald for two and a half years, being gradually entrusted with more responsibility in "Chevrolet traffic"—but not in the creative "Chevrolet copywriting." That would come some years later. But the big Detroit advertising agency opened his eyes, just as the navy had. There he had seen himself as merely one player in a great world drama involving everyone from brass hats to bomber pilots and indigenous peoples being played out against the background of a world conflict.

At Campbell-Ewald, the battle was to sell cars—GM cars—to America. In the navy, Leonard had often wondered how much he was contributing to the destruction of Tojo and Hirohito, cartoonlike figures with thick glasses and buck teeth menacing the world from miles away. But now he could actually see General Motors in action, conducting its fierce campaign. People read ads, bought cars, and made other people rich and successful. Writing was power. The pen really was mightier than the sword. He had seen them both. Now he could even combine them. He knew he was as good or better than the men in the office around him who wrote the ads that sold the cars. He decided he would write stories, the kind that people bought and read, the same people who bought Chevrolets, Pontiacs, and Oldsmobiles, stories for a big audience and probably stories about the sword—or at least the gun—action stories, better written and of better quality than what the competition out there offered, "out there" being the Westerns.

Western Stories

He chose Westerns for several reasons: First, because he had liked those black-and-white movies on Saturday afternoons as a kid, films like *The Plainsman* (1937), *Stagecoach* (1939), *Red River* (1938), and after the war *My Darling Clementine* (1949), elemental tales set in a scenic and dangerous place that never failed to stimulate the imagination. Then, too, in those days the corner stores displayed at least a dozen Western pulps with garish covers of unshaven hard guys firing Peacemakers at men disappearing into saloons or riding off into the cactus. He felt confident he could tell a story as well as the writers who sold to *Dime Western, Western Story,* and *Zane Grey's Western Magazine.*

Leonard has always thrived on challenges, always liked to show that the little guy, the "office boy," the swabbie handing out the beer, could best the big shots every time. Something of this spirit drives him to beat every deadline, to do the unexpected, or to give an unfamiliar twist. For these reasons, he wrote Westerns without cowboys and chose unfamiliar locales and time periods, a habit still with him today when he writes about Israel or Christian stigmatics tangling with traditional liturgists, or fin de siècle Havana in the months after the *Maine* explosion. With characters ranging from mashers to mystics, Leonard never fears to jump headfirst—after he has checked his facts.

Crime Stories

In addition to Westerns, Leonard had read plenty of crime and detective stories, though he bristles today when compared to the hard-boiled school. He offers no "shamuses," no first-person narration; and those early practitioners, dripping decadence and indulging in clever dialogue, full of figurative language, get on his nerves: "Her eyes were shiny black shoe buttons, her cheeks were as soft as suet and about the same color. She was sitting behind a black glass desk that looked like Napoleon's tomb and she was smoking a cigarette in a black holder that was not quite as long as a rolled umbrella."[6] But an unpublished 1950 story of his called "One Horizontal" (later retitled "A Seven Letter Word for Corpse") shows the attraction the Black Mask school had for him. This story, written to be read at a meeting of a Detroit writers club that he stopped attending after a couple of sessions, shows equally the influence of Mickey Spillane, then achieving prominence as the final flowering of the tough-guy-cum-noir style. Leonard's protagonist (who does tell his story in the first person) is tough as nails and makes no concessions to women: "I grabbed her by the wrist. 'Open it, but act nice. ' "[7] In attempting to find his brother's killer, he wanders Detroit's mean streets, a .45 in his raincoat pocket, Leonard having apparently forgotten that a fully loaded Colt automatic weighs as much as several cans of soup.

Starting Out

Although "Trail of the Apache" in *Argosy* had been praised for its
authentic detail, Leonard was convinced that his rejected stories lacked
the utter familiarity with people and locales he so much admired in
Ernest Hemingway's *For Whom the Bell Tolls,* a book that would remain
for years Leonard's bible on the craft of writing. To improve the authenticity of settings, he began to acquire issues of *Arizona Highways* and
started borrowing library books on the Southwest and the Apaches. One
grayish green, cloth-covered notebook he kept during this period contains such notes as "Apaches had an excessive dread of the owl. If it
hooted near camp, it was an omen of frightful import." On another
page, he has copied out "Apaches' favorite meat—mule, horse, then cow.
In that order." And on yet another page of the same notebook appears a
fact destined to reappear a number of times in novels: "Fifth Cavalry
called 'Dandy 5th.' "

From the early fifties onward, Leonard focused on the careful documentation and fidelity to detail that has become a hallmark of his fiction. In later years, he would rely on the assistance of others: first Bill
Marshall, a classmate at the University of Detroit and a detective in
Florida, for details on surveillance, bail bonding, bounty hunting, and a
host of esoteric minutiae; and from about 1981 on, a full-time
researcher, Gregg Sutter, a perceptive writer himself and student of popular culture.

Sutter's job is to research settings, backgrounds, and activities. Neither he nor Leonard makes any apologies for the employment of a full-
time researcher. Sutter compares himself to a batboy or even uses an
archaeological metaphor: "I'm like someone who leads an archaeological
dig, then turns the findings over to someone who knows what they
mean."[8] The thought that another is assisting the writer may make
purists uncomfortable, but the practice is widespread. For centuries,
painters have relied on assistants in the production of canvasses, a practice that causes art historians—not to mention auctioneers—endless
distress. In that respect there is little difference between Leonard and
Leonardo. Writers such as Émile Zola and Theodore Dreiser regularly
sought assistance for the purpose of documenting their fiction.

Leonard is fully aware that each new novel generates decisions in
New York and Hollywood about options and film production money as
well as softcover distribution, foreign rights, the myriad contracts a
movie requires, TV possibilities (including potential serial program-

ming), and so on. He knows he has become a business on whom scores depend and that a business of this magnitude cannot be run single-handedly. A professional researcher like Gregg Sutter is as necessary to Leonard as a law firm.

His documentation grows out of the established conventions of much naturalistic fiction and the simple recognition that specific details lend interest to prose. In his composition and rhetoric courses at college, he had already learned that even drab sentences could be resuscitated with eye-grabbing detail. However, he has developed a kind of second sense for the art of the detail on both the small and the large scale. Above all, he avoids the sense-numbing reveling in details for details' sake in which popular writers such as Ian Fleming sometimes indulge. Leonard successfully conveys to readers the effect that he knows all there is to know about shylocking, bail bonding, casino gambling, and bookmaking even when, as he readily admits, he has no idea what *Pronto*'s Harry Arno's jargon-filled telephone calls from clients mean: "Harry, give me the Lions and the Niners twenty times reverse. Bears a nickel, Chargers a nickel. Giants five times, New England ten times if the Rams ten."[9]

But it had been Leonard's documentation that first caught the eye of Marguerite Harper, who spotted "Trail of the Apache" in the December 1951 issue of *Argosy*. The independent literary agent's complimentary remarks both pleased him and convinced him of her critical insight. Although she already represented several Western pulp writers including Luke Short and Peter Dawson (an issue that became briefly a bone of contention), Leonard accepted her offer to become his agent.

The association of the young writer and the middle-aged agent continued for the next 15 years, spawning a lively correspondence. The self-reliant, honest woman provided Leonard practical lessons in the day-to-day reality of publishing popular fiction. All her letters are self-typed and, though often betraying a slippery knowledge of orthography, reveal a kind heart. In her second letter, signed familiarly "Marguerite" (by the third, she is calling him "Dutch"), she drops a phrase that has since become a byword: "Don't give up your job. . . ." She says that two cents a word is "top for all the pulps" and urges him to set his sights on the *Saturday Evening Post,* one slick that prints Westerns, reminding him that slicks don't "buy by the word" (29 November 1951). Only a month after her first letter offering to be his agent, she was able to sell "Road to Desperation" to *Zane Grey's Western Magazine* for $110. Leonard's check would be $99.90. She crows, "It hasn't taken me too long to get my first sale for you" (24 December 1951).

In his early years at the Campbell-Ewald agency, Leonard showed great dedication to his story writing, designing a disciplined schedule that gave him two hours each morning before leaving for work in addition to stolen moments on the job. So energetically did he labor that Marguerite Harper was able to place nine stories throughout 1952. By 1953, he had sold 10 stories and written *The Bounty Hunters,* which Houghton Mifflin took for $3,000. At the very end of the year, Marguerite Harper wrote him encouragingly as a New Year's wish: "Lets [*sic*] resolve to make some real money from writing. . . . How about ten thousand dollars?" (29 December 1953).

After two and a half years, Leonard left his job at Campbell-Ewald for a 15-month stint at a smaller agency "to learn the advertising business." When he returned to Campbell-Ewald, he was made a full-fledged Chevrolet copywriter and accorded professional status, no more the "office boy" or calling others "mister."

In succeeding years of the decade, Leonard not only turned out a string of Western stories and wrote three more Western novels but answered Hollywood's call. "Three-Ten to Yuma," published in *Dime Western* in 1953, appeared on the screen in 1957. The same studio, Columbia, also produced that year *The Tall T,* made from an *Argosy* story, "The Captives."[10] A story Leonard sold in 1956 to the *Saturday Evening Post,* called "The Waiting Man," (retitled by the *Post* "Moment of Vengeance"), appeared on TV's *Schlitz Playhouse.* Placement in the *Post* had now been realized, and Marguerite Harper told him that the $850 he received would be increased next time to $1,000, advising him: "It means much to get in the *Post*" (26 October 1955).

But times were changing. Television was gobbling up Westerns at the expense of magazines and the movies. The day of the pulps was just about over. In October 1957 Harper told Leonard, "The *Post* editors have decided that westerns have lost their terrific popularity." The next year, she wrote, "everyone is avoiding westerns," although later she states in a characteristically mixed metaphor: "The gold has been killed by TV's abundant supply" (28 September 1958). In January 1960, when Leonard had finished *Hombre,* the tightest and most gripping of his Western novels till then, and was waiting to see it placed, Marguerite Harper wrote bluntly: "You just must switch to some other medium for now" (27 January 1960). Leonard must have gulped hard.

He had both a good job with a prestigious advertising agency and growing status in a writing market that seemed about to collapse. He made a decision—to quit work. The previous year, on a trip to Arizona in connection with some GM pickup truck ads, he had gotten his first look at the Santa Catalina Mountains. Realizing that *Arizona Highways* notwithstanding, his depictions of the mountains bore little resemblance to the real thing, he concluded that the mountains of his stories were as good or better. He realized that his imaginative powers were strong and his creative potential endless.

Taking $11,000 from Campbell-Ewald's profit-sharing plan, he set out to write a book. He figured that the money would take him and his family through half a year, enough time. But a house came on the market they liked, and the move ate up most of the money he had accumulated.

For the next five years, Leonard freelanced, running a handful of accounts he assembled with the assistance of friends and contacts in the advertising business, among these Eaton Chemicals, a manufacturer of dry cleaning products, and Hurst Shifters.

When George Hurst himself had come to Detroit from Warminster, Pennsylvania, to find an advertising agency for his product, revered among stock car and street racers, a colleague of Leonard's saw the opportunity to do him a good turn and convinced the eastern manufacturer that the sort of high-powered Detroit advertising firm he envisioned was all wrong for him. Without a huge budget, his ads would fall to the lowliest copywriters and art directors on the agency totem pole. Instead Hurst should turn to Dutch Leonard.

Leonard, who neither knew what a Hurst Shifter was nor had an office in which to receive Hurst, managed to keep his prospective client at bay while he found out and designed an ad in two days. An elephant foot umbrella stand—a Victorian *tschotschke* of pretentious dwellings—was pressed into service. The ad displayed an elephant's foot about to descend on a Hurst Shifter with the caption "Guaranteed for Life—Unless." Hurst loved it and signed up with Leonard.

Making Movies

In addition to managing several accounts Leonard began to make industrial and educational movies. In his first year on his own, he made more than a half dozen of them with a friend Bill Dineen, an independent film producer. Leonard's initial effort was for the Franciscan Brothers, a Roman Catholic order that wanted a movie to recruit young men. Dineen asked Leonard if he could write the film. Leonard, seldom disconcerted by unfamiliarity with an assignment, accepted and was introduced on a small scale to a new world of making films and writing screenplays. The movie lead, a 30-year-old Franciscan priest who looked 17 (from a missionary outpost on the Amazon) became the inspiration for Juvenal in *Touch* (1987), a novel actually written in 1978.

Together Leonard and Dineen produced a number of movies for Encyclopaedia Britannica Films including *Settlement of the Mississippi Valley, Settlement of the Northwest Territory,* and *Frontier Boy,* 26-minute films making maximum use of photographs, paintings, and voice-overs. "We did *The Danube,"* Leonard recalls, admitting wistfully, "I've never seen the Danube." While making two more of these $10,000 films about the Iberian Peninsula, *Spain* and *Boy of Spain,* the team saw the opportunity to shoot *Julius Caesar,* using the million-dollar sets outside of Madrid left over from Samuel Bronston's recently completed spectacle *The Fall of the Roman Empire.* The only payment demanded by the Hollywood mogul was that Leonard and Dineen sit through a 188-minute screening of the movie with him to watch Sophia Loren, James Mason, and the rest of the cast go through their paces. Unable to find a single redeeming feature in the epic, Leonard could only say to Bronston when the lights came on, "Boy, that was a picture!"

Although Leonard was nagged by the feeling that, having drifted away from his writing goals, he was wasting time, the film experience he gained in the years from 1961 to 1965 would be profitable in the long run, for he learned that he could handle screenplays. After all, he had mastered writing advertising copy, selling short stories and novels in a competitive market, and producing fiction that Hollywood would occasionally buy. Why couldn't he write movies, too? He had always been an avid moviegoer, and though not invited to participate in the two films made from his stories, he followed the process with interest. Further, Hollywood was considering *Hombre,* which Marguerite Harper had sold to Ballantine for $1,250 around the time he left Campbell-Ewald. But for a man who still thought of himself as a writer, it was distressing not to write. When Twentieth Century Fox purchased film rights for *Hombre* for $10,000 in 1965, Leonard renewed the decision he had made more than four years earlier to become a full-time writer.

Back to Writing

He knew he must try something different, to get away from the Westerns, but his attitude toward them remained ambiguous, and he would write two more before leaving them for good.[11] Although still attracted to Westerns, he understood they were considered a subgenre, and that with the exception of a handful of titles such as *The Virginian* or *The Ox-Bow Incident,* they were not considered serious literature. Further, he was aware that in writing them he limited his appeal. Years later he would admit that they had required less than his full potential. Instead, he looked to contemporary Michigan to inspire a novel he was calling *Mother, This Is Jack Ryan.* Just as the Western novels became the laboratory for his themes and techniques, so *Jack Ryan* would for the crime fiction that would establish his reputation.

Jack Ryan of the new novel comes from a Detroit working-class family and finds himself mixed up with 18-year-old Nancy Hayes, a nastier version of Lorraine Kidston of *Last Stand at Saber River.* Together the two commit acts of vandalism in a sleepy resort area on Lake Huron. The story alternates exposition skillfully with dialogue and abounds in swiftly introduced chapters and scenes. But the auctorial exposition, even when presented from a character's point of view, is often stilted. The novel bumps along to an indeterminate conclusion vague enough to puzzle. Perhaps this sort of thing was what that endearing wise guy Chili Palmer had in mind in *Get Shorty* when he said: "Fuckin' endings, man, they weren't as easy as they looked."[12]

The Years with Swanie

Leonard's faithful Marguerite Harper, who was failing physically and mentally by 1966, sent the new manuscript to a West Coast colleague, H. N. Swanson. A colorful old-time Hollywood agent, Swanie had founded *College Humor,* for which such luminaries as Dorothy Parker, Robert Benchley, and Alexander Woolcott had written in the thirties. Now thriving in the movie capital, Swanie represented at times practically every American literary figure with movie connections, from Hemingway, Fitzgerald, and Faulkner to Nathanael West and John O'Hara, and numbered among his friends directors, producers, and actors. When Swanie read *Jack Ryan,* his first words, Leonard says, were "Kiddo, I'm going to make you rich." But it was an uphill battle. Charles Hecklemann's comment at David McKay reflects the editorial basting *Jack Ryan* (now being called *The Big Bounce*) took: "The story is much too long-winded, slow moving, heavily detailed, marred by too many story-slowing flashbacks, and lacking in basic plot substance."[13]

Leonard tried to take into consideration the editorial criticism he found valid, though like so many writers he saw that editors, critics, and readers showed no consistency in their judgments. Nonetheless, he rewrote the book, and Swanson sold it after countless rejections, first to Warner Brothers, then as a Gold Medal Original paperback. Leonard never liked the screenplay done by the producer Bob Dozier and detested the movie. Even before either movie or publishing contracts were signed, Leonard was thinking about taking a Western story about a Mexican American and expanding it to book length, although he had ostensibly abandoned Westerns. Part of the reason for this decision came from the difficulties *Bounce* was encountering; another part was the instinct of an old baseball player to feel it was safer to "tag up" before advancing to another base. Swanie liked what he saw of the new book but was concerned that starting it might steal time from revisions to *Bounce*. Nonetheless, *Valdez Is Coming* was soon finished, and Swanson told Leonard that Burt Lancaster was interested in it. Talk was that Marlon Brando might take a role, too. Although that hope never materialized, film rights were sold for $45,000.

But Leonard already had a new idea for a story about Kentucky and Prohibition and wrote a 10-page outline for it that MGM bought for $50,000 as the first installment of a full-length screenplay—his first. Then he sat down and turned those few pages into a novel he called first *The Broke-Leg War* and later *The Moonshine War*. To Hollywood, the screenplay, completed in the summer of 1968, seemed a good bet to capitalize on the huge success of *Bonnie and Clyde* (1967) of the previous year. Swanie wrote to say: "Any time you decide you want a career as a screenwriter I am ready to run with you."[14]

Next Leonard touched base again with *Forty Lashes Less One* about imaginary events at the Yuma Territorial Prison at the turn of the century. Neither a conventional Western nor crime fiction, the book (a screenplay first) incorporates two themes that appear for the next 30 years: the effect of prison on men and of the mingling of different races and nationalities.

Screenplays

The sale of *The Moonshine War* screenplay by Swanie (who later called Dutch Leonard the "son" that he "never had" in an inscription to his memoir *Sprinkled with Ruby Dust*) served to remind Leonard how deep filmland's pockets really were. From this point on, he would never lose sight of the Hollywood potential in anything he wrote. In fact, he followed *Forty Lashes Less One* and *The Moonshine War* with more screenplays, *The Sun-King Man* and *Jesus Saves,* neither of which was actually made into a movie, and later *Picket Line* and *American Flag,* both with Western settings and both sold but not filmed. *Picket Line* (1971), with a theme of injustice toward itinerant farmworkers, would provide material for *Mr. Majestyk,* another screenplay, filmed with Charles Bronson, that Leonard rewrote as a novel, both appearing in 1974. *Joe Kidd* was bought by Clint Eastwood and released in 1972. Set in the early years of the present century in New Mexico, it stressed Anglo injustice to the Hispanics who had settled in the Southwest long before them. A Mexican American, Luis Chama (ably abetted, of course, by Clint Eastwood) leads a fight against vicious land barons. The Spanish leader of his people had appeared in *Bounty Hunters* and would again in *Gunsights* (1979) in the character of Aviendo Doro, who, while treated with sympathy, emerges in *Gunsights* as a bit of a windbag. Leonard was learning that men and women of color could also be depicted with humor.

Mr. Majestyk appeared under the Dell imprint in 1974, a rousing adventure-thriller with a tough, alienated hero and a topical theme about farmworkers.

These were extraordinarily busy years for Leonard. Hollywood was building his bank account, but the social drinking he had enthusiastically indulged in since navy days was crowding his life, and his marriage to Beverly was coming apart. A turning point of another sort was around the corner, though. He was about to publish *52 Pick-Up.*

More than any other novel, *52 Pick-Up* (1974) established Leonard's direction for the next two decades, for despite his achievements in the Western and his experiments with historical adventure stories such as *The Moonshine War* and *Cuba Libre,* his name and reputation are now inextricably bound to crime fiction and seem likely to remain so—to books such as *LaBrava* (1983), *Glitz* (1985), *Freaky Deaky* (1988), *Rum Punch* (1992), and *Riding the Rap* (1995). Critics and reviewers of the eighties who began taking notice of Leonard invariably compared him to the noir detective writers of the twenties and thirties on the basis of books in the spirit of *52 Pick-Up,* not *The Hunted* (1977) or *Touch* (1987), let alone the Westerns, of which few were even aware.

And though Leonard balks, the critics are more right than wrong, because he writes best—albeit with mordant humor—of a dark, multiracial America, a country of gloomy or sunbaked cities where values are minimal and psychotics lurk at every turn, where betrayal and dysfunction are norms, where the violent prey on the weak, and crime is one way of making a living.

In 1972 H. N. Swanson, who almost never mentions literature as anything but a "property"—despite his letterhead "Writers and Writings"—had written to Leonard: "I think you might want to read a new book just published, *The Friends of Eddie Coyle* by George V. Higgins. Has fine dialogue and underworld characters. Very heavy, as they say on the strip." Leonard took his advice to heart, and *Friends* became what *For Whom the Bell Tolls* had been for so many years, another enchiridion.

In *52 Pick-Up,* Leonard wrote for the first time about downtown Detroit and its nearby suburbs. He assigned a prominent role to a black figure, the small-time pimp and hood Bobby Shy, who speaks a laid-back cool black English, dropping articles and verbs in a fashion influenced by Higgins. "Feel free to give my assistant your wallets, billfolds, money belts, watches, jewelry. I mean don't hold back, 'cause we robbing the stagecoach, friends, taking everything you got." In addition, Leonard's language became saltier after reading Higgins, and the "shits" and "motherfuckers" he had had to avoid in more restrictive times grew frequent.

He jumped about more, moving into scenes confidently, letting his characters' speech make clear to the reader who was talking and what was going on. He began manipulating the devices that would become associated with his name: the elaborate caper often involving a large sum of money (in *52 Pick-Up* it starts off as $52,000); the psychotic or sociopathic characters (Bobby Shy and Alan Raimy, heirs to Elisha Cook Jr. and Richard Widmark); the involved plots that at first glance seem flawless but on closer examination reveal inconsistencies. Although no detective puts in an appearance, the protagonist, Harry Mitchell, displays uncanny powers of observation and deduction:

> "You said 'I guess you have the same problems in your business, absenteeism and so on.'"
> "Yeah?"
> "How did you know what business I'm in?"[15]

Also in *52 Pick-Up,* Leonard shows a keen satiric gift in his depiction of the vacuity and hypocrisy of American life, a society where wealth rubs shoulders with poverty, and nude photo studios and porno theaters are accepted features of the urban landscape, where even the decent Harry Mitchell cheats on his wife, and the blackmailers turn on each other without a second thought.

Swag (1976) maintained the pace, though it was less graphic. It offers the same quick transitions and the careful point of view in which the narrator maintains his distance, allowing the characters to speak for themselves. *Swag* also presents great cop talk scenes influenced by George V. Higgins showing insiders cynically discussing opportunities for criminal conviction in a system full of compromise. For example, a white Detroit detective and a black prosecutor scheme over lunch how best to nab Frank Ryan and Ernest Stickley for a major crime they have committed. The plan involves betrayal, turning gang members against each other. The prosecutor suggests that the detective

> "make him realize life can be dangerous out there. Man disappears for a time, they find him in the trunk of a car out at the airport. Say to him he ought to be very careful where he goes, where he meets his friends."
>
> "Yeah," Cal said, "get him to reconsider who his friends are, who can do him the most good."
>
> "That's it." Emory Parks smiled then. "You're going to take all this back to Thirteen Hundred and Walter's going to say, 'You've been talking to that fat little nigger again, haven't you?' and you'll say, 'Well, I just picked at his brain a little.' "[16]

This sort of thing, the cops outwitting the bad guys over lunch, is pure Higgins, but Leonard makes it his own, a hallmark of his fiction so convincing that an instructor at the John Jay School of Criminal Justice wrote him to say he uses the scene in his classes.[17]

Leonard was dazzled by Higgins's dialogue. Higgins's talk seemed truer to life than any Leonard had previously seen, with its absent conjunctions, vague pronoun references, and pregnant cul-de-sacs effortlessly advancing the narration in a fashion for which he had been striving. Higgins's hapless losers and sleazy third-rate underworld groupies were the same people who had been attracting Leonard's interest. Like Walt Whitman, who said he had been simmering till Emerson brought him to a boil, Leonard found that Higgins got him boiling.

In 1974 Leonard found himself dealing with an Israeli film production company that had bought the rights to *52 Pick-Up*. In the midst of his drinking years, he welcomed the invitation to visit the Near East to advise Noah Films Limited and to do some imbibing away from censorious eyes. Later he would say that for bibulous activity, Dublin would have been a better choice than Tel Aviv or Jerusalem.

The trip, however, resulted in *The Hunted* (1977), which despite a contemporary foreign setting is largely another Western, Arizona as much as Israel. David E. Davis ("the marine") and Tali, the Israeli girl, are really Gary Cooper and Ingrid Bergman from *For Whom the Bell Tolls*, and the talk about hotels owes to the Pamplona scenes of *The Sun Also Rises*.

In his next two novels, *Unknown Man # 89* (1977) and *The Switch* (1978), Leonard returned to Detroit. The first of these reintroduces Frank Ryan of *The Big Bounce,* pitting him against F. X. Perez, whose antecedents lie in Sydney Greenstreet in *The Maltese Falcon* (1941). *Unknown Man # 89* is a gripping crime story with wonderful black characters—one called Tunafish is worth the price of admission alone— and contains a quick side trip to Florida, a setting Leonard would turn to more in years to come. Much of the novel, however, seems a bit dated with its late-Woodstock lingo, a good deal of it apparently attributable to Leonard's experiences in Alcoholics Anonymous as he struggled to get off the bottle. People are continually being urged to feel good about themselves and build self-esteem through the type of tough love encountered at AA meetings and kaffeeklatsches.

That same year, he wrote the remarkable *Touch,* which had to wait another decade for publication, though it was once optioned for the screen by Bruce Willis and actually appeared as a movie in selected American cities in 1996. A number of Leonard's personal experiences as a recovering alcoholic transform the book into an act of thanksgiving. Despite light touches and perceptive satire, *Touch* differs from his other novels and has proved less popular. But in writing it, he ran true to form in that he both changed direction and retreated to familiar territory before venturing forth again with renewed confidence.

The Switch is a variation on *52 Pick-Up,* another Detroit couple and another kidnapping for ransom. Leonard prophetically invents a neo-Nazi who bears an uncanny resemblance to Richard Jewell, whom the FBI later suspected of the Atlanta Olympic Games bombing. The female lead, Leonard claims, was modeled on his second wife, Joan.

The decade of the seventies concludes with Leonard turning once again to a Western in a fashion that had almost become a pattern. *Gun-sights* (1979) is his novelistic farewell to the genre, set in the last years of the previous century. David Geherin astutely compares the novel to Stephen Crane's "The Bride Comes to Yellow Sky," itself clearly an influence on *High Noon* (1952), a favorite Leonard film.

The seventies neatly bracket, too, what might be called either "the early phase" or "the middle years," depending on how we choose to look at it. As far as the American reading public was concerned, the earlier term would be the more accurate. Leonard had completed an apprenticeship of nearly 30 years and was beginning to attract recognition—

beginning. From his own perspective, "the middle years" would make more sense. He had said good-bye to the Western novel (though with fingers crossed) and poured down his last drink—"I think it was a Scotch and ginger ale," he told *People* magazine in 1985, with his Amazing Kreskin–like memory.

In 1977, the year he quit drinking for good, he was divorced from his wife, Beverly Cline, mother of his five children. Leonard and Beverly had separated in 1974. Within two years, he married Joan Shepard, who died of cancer in 1993. At this point, the bulk of Leonard's earnings was coming from film contracts, though he was establishing himself as a regional writer of crime fiction and was on his way to becoming "the Dickens of Detroit," as *Time* would dub him, though calling him the Hogarth might be more accurate.

In these years, he found that he would need help in continuing to provide the sort of documented details that lend authenticity to his books. Thus it is not surprising that when the *Detroit News* asked him in 1978 to write an article about the city's police, he headed straight for 1300 Beaubien, police headquarters, an address he had often mentioned in his books.

Instead of a few days of observation, his visit turned into months of nights and days in squad rooms and on the streets. During this period, he made valuable contacts, finding several officers he could call up later to query about points of police procedure. He liked many of the men he met and found that their opponents, the crooks, were pretty dumb, as he had always imagined. The worse they were, the dumber they seemed to be. He was impressed by the orderliness of the squad room and later insisted that the TV series *Barney Miller* and Ed McBain's 87th Precinct novels presented a more accurate picture of police at work than the orchestrated chaos of *Hill Street Blues* or *NYPD Blue*. And he was gratified to discover that the world he had envisioned, the language and the behavior he had created in his novels, differed little from the real thing, that he had been as successful in imagining the squad room as he had been in recreating the adjutant's room in an Arizona territorial outpost or an engineer's office in a western copper town. The schemes and deals hadn't changed much, either.

The success of the police in the face of heavy odds won Leonard's admiration, though he was not sure how much of that success was achieved because of criminal stupidity and how much because a moral force in the universe seemed to assert itself from time to time to the advantage of the dedicated and persevering people who pursued cases, often bad-humoredly, but doggedly and efficiently. He watched men and women of different social classes, races, and ethnic origins working together because they knew they must in the hodgepodge of modern, multicultural America, and he saw a comic potential in the disparities he witnessed. Police and criminals alike struggled to bring their behavior in line with dimly perceived norms. Imposed standards that they did not understand but recognized as being socially approved produced all sorts of wildly funny aberrations in an America of conflicting values. But Leonard himself is nonjudgmental. In depicting his characters he presents their views from their perspectives so consistently that readers are obliged to take these figures seriously even when they are hilariously off course.

The Eighties

With *Gunsights,* ostensibly his last Western, behind him, Leonard did not attempt to take immediate advantage of his 1300 Beaubien experience but instead launched forth in a new direction. Next he wrote *Gold Coast* (1980), which was published after *City Primeval* (1980), though actually predating it in composition. For *Gold Coast,* he chose for the first time a setting in Florida, where his mother owned a small, unprofitable motel, and where he had been vacationing for years. The characters in this novel are largely Detroit transplants, but the new setting works well—though a woman's identification of herself with Bugsy Siegel's old girlfriend Virginia Hill baffles.

City Primeval, with its noir title and mood, draws directly on Leonard's weeks at Detroit's police headquarters but still manages to give vent to a satirical strain, a shoulder-shrugging observation of the zany extremities of American life that becomes a hallmark from *52 Pick-Up* on. *City Primeval* also marks a new development in Leonard's career as a professional writer, for he had been growing increasingly frustrated with lack of recognition, feeling that for one who had been on the scene for so long, book sales were not what they should be. But just as he finished this riveting and violent story of contemporary Detroit, he was approached by Donald Fine, a pioneer in the promotion of the new hardcover-softcover concept in publishing by which both rights were bought at once to new books.

Fine, a Harvard graduate three years older than Leonard, and notoriously hot-tempered, had been born in nearby Ann Arbor and attended the Cranbrook School in Bloomfield Hills. In fact, he had been Leonard's editor at Dell when he published *Last Stand at Saber River* and one of the founders of Delacorte Press, which Leonard felt had failed, like Bantam, to bring him to the attention of the American public. But Fine had left Delacorte in 1969 to open his own company, Arbor House, and had since had a number of publishing successes, including Ken Follett's blockbuster *The Eye of the Needle* (1978). Although Fine had sold Arbor House to the Hearst Corporation for $1.5 million, he remained as president of the company, and now he promised Leonard that what he had been able to do for authors like John MacDonald he could do for Leonard: "We'll create a whole new Elmore Leonard reputation."[18] Fine meant that he would see that Leonard's work reached important reviewers.

Leonard was in a mood to listen, aware that he was still "virtually unknown outside the city [Detroit]. And for that matter not too well known in Detroit either."[19] To be sure, Leonard's reviews could have been more plentiful, but Newgate Callendar in the *New York Times* had been an important exception. The pseudonymous crime fiction and detective story reviewer (revealed years later to be the *Times*'s music critic Harold Schonberg) regularly wrote enthusiastic notices that had a clout far out of proportion to their brevity.

Donald Fine probably suggested that Leonard could profit from a trick or two from the bag of Arbor House's cynosure John MacDonald, an enthusiastic new Leonard admirer. One device, going back to Poe and Conan Doyle, was to use a larger-than-life reappearing central figure whom readers got to know and looked for book after book. Leonard, of course, had nothing like that. He had none of the other gimmicks either: no familiar, repeated settings—beyond Florida and Detroit—such as a police precinct or familiar haunts, no attention-catching titles, part of some sort of established series featuring a color, an initial letter, or even a day of the week.

He was not exactly receptive to any of these ideas. Part of the problem arose from the fact that he has never fully accepted being pigeonholed as a crime writer. Rather, he considers himself a novelist who uses suspense and writes about characters whose lives involve them with crime. Consequently, he was hesitant to proceed in the direction of an Ed McBain, Donald Westlake, John MacDonald, Harry Kemelman, or Sue Grafton, though he knew the rubric of "detective story" was now regularly used to designate his work, too. Nor did he want to be locked into the big-city police story, essentially what *City Primeval* was, and he felt a bit uncomfortable with the noir air that book projected, one smacking of metaphors, adverbs, and convoluted solutions to melodramatic murders—all things he insisted did not belong to the Leonard style, a style he was starting to identify more in terms of a "sound." His books, he felt, had an identifiable voice, contemporary, gritty, unsentimental, and unlike the pages of others, especially those early writers to whom he was always being compared.

Thus he found himself for a short time torn between adopting some of the successful formulas of others and going his own way. But Leonard has never been one to agonize long about writing decisions, believing more problems lurk for those inclined to stop and find them. He decided to make use of more of the colorful details and documentation he had acquired with the Detroit Police and to bring back Detective Raymond Cruz of *City Primeval* for a second appearance, an attempt at continuity that might provide new appeal.

This scheme, unfortunately, did not work. *Split Images* (1981), meant to continue the story of a dedicated Detroit cop, had to be considerably revised when Leonard learned that the name and character of Raymond Cruz were the sole property of United Artists, which had bought film rights to *City Primeval*. Leonard was obliged to go back through the book, making scores of changes as Raymond Cruz turned into Bryan Hurd.

But the new book gave him the opportunity to use Florida settings again. Captivated by the variety of nationalities in southern Florida and its hedonistic lifestyles, Leonard simply packed up his Detroiters, as he had briefly in *Gold Coast,* and sent them off to the Sunshine State without apology, so that *Split Images* is much less a Detroit story than its predecessor. In this novel, too, he took the unusual step of killing off a woman who was a major sympathetic character, something he had not done since *Hombre,* two decades earlier. And although United Artists announced some months later it would film the book as *Hang Tough* to be directed by Sam Peckinpah, nothing came of the project.

Not wanting to get stuck with cop stories, but comfortable with the South Florida setting and the pervasive Caribbean influence of Dade County, Leonard next decided to move his cast between Miami and the Dominican Republic. *Cat Chaser* (1982), published to good reviews only five months after *Split Images,* is the story of George Moran, who returns to the island where he had served as a marine when the United States marched in in 1965. George now owns a motel in Florida, as Leonard's mother did, has a divorce behind him, as Leonard did, and is hung up on the memory of Luci Palma, a guerrilla girl who may still be Ingrid

Bergman. Back in Miami, Moran gets involved with Jiggs Scully, an Irish ex-cop from New York whose skulduggery so endeared him to Leonard that Scully's role grew ever more prominent—something the author admits often occurs—and discredits the belief that he works out every detail before a novel takes shape.

In 1983 Leonard published two novels, *Stick* and *LaBrava,* both garnering the enthusiastic notices he was beginning to consider normal. After the phenomenal success of *Glitz* (1985), *Stick* would bring in $350,000 in movie rights. Ironically, much of the novel deals with a Hollywood producer of schlock films who attempts to finance his latest venture with drug money. In real life, Burt Reynolds produced and starred in the film version, which Leonard hated so much that his name was eventually taken off the credits entirely. Reynolds sensationalized the story, introducing a terrarium full of tarantulas that crawl around as Ernest Stickley cleans house with bursts of gunfire. *LaBrava,* too, displayed Leonard's interest in moviemaking, not as in *Stick* with schemes about how movies are financed, produced, and cast but in Hollywood's noir age. The *New York Times* touted *LaBrava* enthusiastically, and *Newsweek* called the novel "well-paced and plotted, keenly observed and lightly witty with a firm sense of character and place."[20] The Mystery Writers of America awarded it an Edgar as the best crime novel of the year, and additional favorable reviews came from Christopher Lehmann-Haupt in the *New York Times* ("His dialogue is so authentic that it dances off the page") and rival Donald Westlake ("Have I got a book for you").[21] Also, *Times* book critic Herbert Mitgang bestowed national recognition on Leonard in an 800-word article beginning: "After writing 23 novels, Elmore Leonard has been discovered."[22] Calling his work "something special," Mitgang elevated Leonard from the herd of "mystery-suspense" writers, saying that from this point on Leonard was to be considered a "novelist." Mitgang provided a biographical sketch in which Leonard explained how he tries "to get the right people assembled, give them right-sounding names, and then [is] off and running." In guileless fashion, Leonard asserted as so often that his characters lead lives of their own: "I don't know which way it's going to turn out— which character is going to come out of the house alive."

Reviewers, however, continued to call Leonard the heir of Dashiell Hammett and James Cain, pointing at *LaBrava*'s sleazy hotels and nocturnal settings, elements that returned in *Glitz.* Thus, while elated with his new recognition, he continued to chafe at the noir association, dismissing it as a failure of the critical imagination. In this judgment, he has a point, for aside from obvious similarities—chiefly a proclivity for the depiction of dysfunction and betrayal—his fiction eschews the darkness, paranoia, and nihilism that are the real hallmarks of the noir.

If *LaBrava* turned heads, *Glitz* changed everything, generating full treatment of Leonard's work by *Time* and *Gentlemen's Quarterly,* and marking another one of those dramatic turning points in his career that stand out in hindsight.[23] *LaBrava* had sold 20,000 copies in hardcover; *Glitz* sold 10 times as many and spent 16 weeks on the *Times* best-seller list, the first of his books to reach it. Now Leonard, whose annual income in 1983 had been just shy of a million dollars, suddenly soared on by the magic number with *Glitz*'s advances, royalties, film and paperback rights, and payments from the Book-of-the-Month Club.

Glitz had come about in an odd way. While working on a screenplay for *LaBrava,* Leonard had received from producer Walter Mirisch a completed script of a sequel to *In the Heat of the Night* (1967) for tinkering. Actors Rod Steiger and Sidney Poitier would team up again to solve a murder. Leonard considered several settings and looked into a number of prominent murder cases before sending Gregg Sutter out to research Atlantic City and its casinos. Eventually Poitier lost interest in the project but Leonard salvaged great chunks of work for *Glitz.* Yet *Glitz* is not vastly different from other earlier efforts. It features another straight-arrow protagonist and another Richard Widmark–like villain.

Eye-catching settings of *Glitz* show Gregg Sutter's detailed research into Atlantic City, from its cops to "the mob, prostitution, bikers, drugs, gambling, real estate, Puerto Ricans, and submarine sandwiches." Sutter found the town "not much different from Detroit. . . . Glitter and flash covering up a lot of decay, poverty, and despair."[24] *Glitz* draws on Puerto Rico, too, where Leonard had recently vacationed, and the novel provides a satisfying overview of spots in and around San Juan, including the El Yunque rain forest, where the vicious Teddy Magyk does in a hapless cab driver.

Now "the hottest writer in America was profiled in *Rolling Stone* and *People* magazine; his picture appeared on the cover of *Newsweek;* he was invited to appear on the Phil Donahue show; George Will devoted his nationally syndicated column to him; Pete Hamill wrote about him in the *New York Daily News* magazine; *Chicago Tribune* columnist Bob Greene devoted not one but two columns to his work" (Geherin, 16). The tenor of the *Glitz* reviews can be gauged by Stephen King's assertion that it is "the kind of book that if you get up to see if there are any chocolate chip cookies left you take it with you so you won't miss anything."[25]

Before the end of the decade, Leonard published four more books, three in $4.5 million deals with Delacorte. *Touch,* bought back from Bantam by Leonard and published on the strength of *Glitz,* and *Bandits* (1987) have not attained the status of favorites among Leonard fans, probably because of the moral earnestness of each. *Freaky Deaky* is a different story. Leonard's favorite, it features Donnell Lewis, a sort of criminal version of Jeeves the butler. Originally projected as "the heavy," Donnell becomes ever less menacing as Leonard's affection for him grows.

On the heels of *Freaky Deaky,* another title for which his publisher had paid a $1.5 million advance, came *Killshot.* An exciting and suspenseful story set mostly in Michigan of a couple threatened by a murderous pair of criminals, *Killshot* reached the *New York Times* best-seller list the year after *Freaky Deaky.* The book contains a wonderful vignette of a middle-aged Elvis-worshiping woman and authentic scenes of work on high steel and life as a Mississippi bargeman today. *Killshot* builds to a rousing climax when the female protagonist discovers the enemy is inside her house, an elemental fear that has raised the hairs on the back of the neck since "Goldilocks."

The Nineties

If everything changed with *Glitz* in 1985 and stayed changed for the next five years or so, it all happened a second time, not with the book *Get Shorty* (1990) but with the movie in 1995. A new wave of popular recognition not so much increased book sales as maintained them at slightly more than 100,000 copies each.[26] *Get Shorty* received similar bids from publishers with offers from William Morrow and from Delacorte, promising in addition to $1.5 million a contract for two more novels.

Get Shorty and its sequel, *Be Cool* (1999), chronicle the adventures of Chili Palmer, a former loan shark who has cinematic ambitions. The first novel sees him attempting to get a movie produced. Chili's experiences in filmland draw on Leonard's own, particularly with the pint-sized prima donna Michael Weir, based on Dustin Hoffman, who vacillated for months before rejecting the lead role in a projected *LaBrava. Be Cool,* written with screen possibilities at the front of his mind, showcases Leonard's wide knowledge of pop music from Aerosmith to Led Zeppelin—not something most 70 year olds possess. Carefully researched as usual with Gregg Sutter, this book about crooks and the music industry offers endless opportunities as a film to show groups performing, making it particularly appealing to young audiences. John Travolta's salary demands for a second go at the role of Chili Palmer (more than $20 million) and Leonard's price for rights (a modest $1 million) will be some factors in the book's screen future.

For the year after *Get Shorty*, Leonard had ready *Maximum Bob*, as usual well inside his self-imposed deadline. In this violent and funny book about a hanging judge in Florida, he introduces Elvin Crowe (the brother of Roland Crowe of *Gold Coast*), a whacko psychopath. The white-trash Crowes and the womanizing southern judge proved irresistible not only to readers but eventually to TV, which clumsily turned Leonard's inimitable characters into felonious versions of Ma and Pa Kettle.

Rum Punch (1992) concluded his second book deal with Delacorte and took only three years to reach cinemas as *Jackie Brown*, directed by Quentin Tarantino. Made for $15 million, the movie continues to gross profits well in excess of production costs. To document scenes for it in a women's prison, Leonard inspected the Stockade in West Palm Beach during a visit arranged by Judge Marvin Mounts, who partially inspired the politically incorrect Bob Gibbs of *Maximum Bob*.

With his next two novels, *Pronto* and its sequel *Riding the Rap*, Leonard continued the book-a-year pace he foresees as long as he can make the *Times* best-seller list—or, at the worst, those of the *Washington Post* or *Los Angeles Times*. Both novels feature Harry Arno, a character Leonard loves and hates. A breezy, self-made guy who, at an age others seek the rocking chair, still runs a profitable bookmaking operation and has a girlfriend decades younger than he is, Harry is also a loquacious egotist and often a crashing bore. As he grows progressively more stubborn and ungrateful, Leonard loses patience with him, just as he did with a similar character, Al Rosen in *The Hunted*. Once Harry leaves Miami Beach for Rapallo, Italy, the focus shifts to Deputy Marshal Raylan Givens of Harlan County, Kentucky, a slow-to-anger Gary Cooper type but never at a loss for words.

Leonard had been visiting his Italian publisher in Milan, and on a side trip to Rapallo, the notion occurred to him to take Harry and his friends there, too, just as he had done before with settings in Israel, Puerto Rico, and the Dominican Republic. Needing a title, he simply chose the word (meaningless in the novel) that Italians use to answer the phone, *pronto*. *Pronto* contains all the Leonard hallmarks, the breathless confrontations, suspenseful shoot-outs, and quirky characters and situations that lift his stories above those of others.

Riding the Rap (1995) continues Harry's saga, making use of another of those huge Florida waterfront houses that readers know from *Gold Coast* and *Stick*—but this one as messy as Woody Ricks's Detroit mansion in *Freaky Deaky*. Chip Ganz, the villain, is a strung-out version of Robbie Daniels, and his men-of-color flunkies who rode the rap together at Starke are no more gifted kidnappers than were Ordell Robbie and Louis Gara.

Wearing his Western hat and boots, Raylan Givens plays a major role in *Rap*, though his romance with Joyce, begun so promisingly in *Pronto*, fizzles. Harry Arno is back in South Beach, having given up ideas of retirement, but his role is peripheral. Early on he is kidnapped on orders from Chip, who knows that most snatches go awry when it comes to the ransom, something the criminal element of *52 Pick-Up* and *The Switch* had not grasped. Chip's twist will be to negotiate the amount with Harry and then require him to come up with a foolproof method of payment.

Raylan Givens owes a bit to Gary Cooper and a bit more to Clint Eastwood's update of Gary Cooper in roles like Coogan and Dirty Harry, and there are two or three old-fashioned showdowns in the quick-draw tradition, but the total effect of *Riding the Rap* is strictly contemporary. Pages of in-your-face dialogue and brief fragments encapsulating a character's assessment of another, "that cop way of talking," fairly zing. Leonard's prose grows even leaner: "Definite articles drop out, as do adjectives and pronouns; everything occurs in a rolling, improvised present tense."[27]

Leonard's 34th novel, *Out of Sight,* may well be his best to date, and almost as good in its film version as *Get Shorty*. The idea for Karen Sisco, the lead female character, came from a photograph he saw in the *Detroit News* of U.S. Marshal Anna Garza guarding drug defendants in Florida with a pump shotgun resting on one hip and carrying a shoulder bag. Although she doesn't differ greatly from tough and self-reliant heroines such as Kathy Diaz Baker in *Maximum Bob,* Karen displays questionable judgment when it comes to taste in men. A sexy tomboy, a daddy's girl who knows batting averages and boxing records, Karen fails to heed her dad only when he tries to warn her about males, in this case her current beau, Ray:

> "He's still married though, huh?"
> "Technically. They're separated."
> "Oh, he's moved out?"

"He's about to."
"Then they're not separated, are they?"[28]

The true object of her affections turns out to be Jack Foley, a laid-back Louisiana-born bank robber 20 years her senior who suffers his own lacunae in judgment. Karen and Jack meet when he busts out of Glades Correctional Institute, emerging from an escape tunnel dressed as a guard. In short order, he is sharing the trunk of a pal's getaway car with Karen, who has stumbled onto the scene.

The escaped con talking movies with his hostage in the dark brought waves of laughter from a large audience when Leonard read the episode aloud at Barnes and Noble in New York during a publicity tour in the early fall of 1996.

Jack Foley is a cool guy, but when he gets involved with Glenn Michaels and Snoopy Miller, we know he's headed for another fall. The combination of real comedy and convincing criminals receives an added fillip in the form of a romance reminiscent of Hollywood's late-thirties "screwball comedies." Leonard sketches a May-December relationship between two people who know it cannot last. One of the book's best scenes occurs in a cocktail lounge of Detroit's Renaissance Center during a winter storm. After several eager ad men have tried hitting on Karen in vain, Jack arrives "in his neat navy-blue suit, his hair not quite combed but looking great" (*Out of Sight,* 207). In a moment, the two are involved in a fantasy over drinks, he as "Gary" and she "Celeste," high above the silent city. As the stillborn day turns to night, his age and destiny intensify her feelings, for him until they reach the pitch of a Shakespeare sonnet, a "love more strong to love that well which . . . [she] must leave ere long."

As so often-before, Leonard turned backward after *Out of Sight* to an earlier genre in *Cuba Libre,* a novel about the Spanish-American War, finished in the spring of 1997 but published quite by coincidence in the centennial year of that conflict. For all practical purposes, *Cuba Libre* is another Western—as Leonard admits, another novel influenced by *For Whom the Bell Tolls.* Not only did Ben Tyler once work for Dana Moon back in the Arizona Territory, but he touches his hat to ladies in Gary Cooper fashion and falls in love with Celia Brown, a woman with a past who wears her hair cropped when she rides with guerrillas, like Ingrid Bergman. The two bed down in the open on pine needles amid talk of dynamiting a bridge like Robert Jordan and Maria and are soon involved in a train attack like the one in *Forty Lashes Less One,* written a quarter of a century earlier.

A historical novel, *Cuba Libre* is studded with references to real figures and events, ranging from Richard Harding Davis and Stephen
Crane, who covered the war, to Clara Barton and the *Maine* controversy,
much of which Leonard found in Frank Freidel's illustrated history *The
Splendid Little War* and picture books such as *Our Islands and Their People*.
In addition to historical sources, Leonard drew on family stories about
life in Louisiana before his birth and tales about his grandfather's experiences managing a sugar mill in Honduras.

As a "Western," *Cuba Libre* sacrifices the humor and street-smart dialogue of the crime fiction, though the violence remains. (Ben Tyler com-
plains once that he's had to shoot eight men since arriving in Cuba.)
Psychological insights are fewer, and heroics larger than life in this
escapist tale of a kidnapping with a twist, set against an exotic tropical
background in wartime.

Although *Cuba Libre* is not what Leonard fans had become accustomed to, the book reached best-seller status and kept its position on
and off for about four weeks, inducing Universal to buy rights for $3
million. At the moment, the Coen brothers seem likely to make the
movie, over which Leonard has maintained approval rights for choice of
both director and writer.

Well into his seventies, Dutch Leonard lives an abstemious but hardly
monastic life with his third wife, Christine Kent, in an elegant home in
Detroit's poshest suburb, enjoying a variety of interests and keeping up
with the world around him in a fashion few septuagenarians can equal.
He smokes moderately, answers his own telephone, often agreeing to
requests for appearances after checking his calendar, and looks forward
to an Elton John concert at Detroit's Palace (where Elton John will
speak to him personally before jetting back to Atlanta).

He is remarkably at peace with himself and content with the position
he has achieved. He reads widely and is generous in approval of fellow
writers, delighted, for example, with the volumes they often send him,
like those dedicated and signed by Andre Dubus. Leonard is extremely
pragmatic and businesslike in his approach to writing. Although he
shares actively in negotiation discussions, he leaves money talk to agents
and lawyers. Like most writers, he knows exactly how many words fit on
a page or into a chapter, and he writes by hand on specially ordered yellow paper before retyping himself and handing finished chapters to his
daughter to retype. He is happiest when writing, finding almost no difficulty in putting aside long hours each day when working on a book,
and is never bothered by writer's block, though he confessed to feeling

antsy that he had finished *Be Cool,* the sequel to *Get Shorty,* in April 1998 and had yet to begin its successor in early fall of 1998. He had, however, started the Africa research the new book required and worked out the basic elements of its plot.

His enviable equanimity he attributes to his escape years ago from alcoholism through AA. Like so many who have gone through the program, he credits its spiritual dimensions unabashedly, and he appears very little like an Elmore Leonard character—unless Juvenal or Jack Ryan—when he attributes his peace of mind, success, and prosperity to the grace of God. Told that he even sounds a bit like the flashy black evangelist Reverend Ike, who teaches that money is evidence of God's approval, Leonard grins widely. "Money is just a way of keeping score," he says.

Somehow, Dutch Leonard has combined the Protestant work ethic with the Catholic monastic ideal until he's not sure whether to labor is to pray, or doing what God wants just brings big rewards. But in either case, it works for him, and readers all over the globe rejoice that it does.

Chapter Two

Fenimore Cooper to Gary Cooper: Leonard Is Coming

Antecedents of the Western

The Western may conveniently be thought of as beginning with James Fenimore Cooper (1789–1851)—though his *Leatherstocking Tales* might better be called "Easterns," since with the exception of *The Prairie* (1827), these stories of Indians and the scout Natty Bumppo have settings in New York State. The Western is an exclusively American genre, for even when it exists in other countries, it purports to be American and is set in America. Only in rare instances has the Western achieved respectability abroad. An example might be the work of Karl May (1842–1912), an author whom Hitler read enthusiastically. For the most part, the Western's readership is male, and its accomplishments, well beyond the pale of literary fiction, are largely limited to media such as comic books and pulp magazines.

Curiously, however, the Western is roughly the same age as the detective or police story, if we credit Edgar Allan Poe (1809–1849) as its originator with tales of deduction such as "The Murders in the Rue Morgue" (1841) and "The Purloined Letter" (1845), both featuring the eccentric detective C. Auguste Dupin, who would inspire Arthur Conan Doyle's Sherlock Holmes. After Holmes, the detective story proliferates in various evolutions, often existing side by side with the Western, and sharing many of its conventions until the fifties, when the detective story pulls ahead. Whatever the future of the detective story may be, it seems destined to flourish beyond the Western.

Thus it is not surprising that Leonard, always a commercial writer, shifted from one type of genre fiction to another. Readily adaptable to all countries and more appealing to readers worldwide, the crime story is more flexible. American crime stories have been popular in Great Britain for years, and British stories sell well in the United States and other English-speaking countries. Further, unlike the Western, which has attracted very few women writers, the crime story has called forth many, ranging from Agatha Christie, who works in what Poe called the "ratiocinative" mode (in which a mystery is solved), to Joyce Carol Oates, whose stories (like those of so many of her contemporaries) draw metaphorically on the violent activity that fills the pages of our newspapers and TV screens on the eleven o'clock news.

The Western has proved less adaptable for a variety of reasons. Primarily, it is a historical novel set in a remote area during the years from the end of the Civil War to the conclusion of the Indian campaigns (chiefly those against Geronimo, ending when his band of Chiricahua Apaches was sent into exile from Fort Bowie in the Arizona Territory in September 1886, or the Sioux uprising of 1890, culminating in the massacre at Wounded Knee).

As a historical novel, the Western is subject to restrictions of accuracy and authenticity. Not only is it limited in setting and time, but it must adhere to nebulous rules about which little agreement exists. Some would claim that a Western living experience is a necessity; others, that cowboys or Indians must be characters. Leonard often writes about Indians but seldom about cowboys, and he has never lived for an extended period of time in the Southwest he depicts.

Usually the Western features a single hero, but Leonard experiments with this convention regularly. His stories alternate between those like *The Bounty Hunters* (1953), in which Dave Flynn and Duane Bowers share the stage, and his novel of the next year, *The Law at Randado,* with Kirby Frye as its main figure. Leonard found that he could handle either situation comfortably, and he continued to alternate methods after leaving the Western, though he consistently returns to one figure in his narration like a switch-hitter favoring one side. Sometimes his choice seems motivated by the memory of a book, or more often a movie, as demonstrated by the inspiration of *Shane* (1953) on *Last Stand at Saber River,* or Gary Cooper's role in *High Noon* (1952) on *3:10 to Yuma.*

For a long time, Gary Cooper remained the standard by which Leonard measured his ideal taciturn man of action. Cooper and costar Ingrid Bergman and *For Whom the Bell Tolls*—both the novel and the movie—got into Leonard's blood so thoroughly that their influences remain strong to this day. He adopted not only symbolic devices such as the purity of the high country as opposed to the tainted low ground but also the tradition of local color. Hemingway's gypsy men and peasant women (the legacy of writers such as Prosper Mérimée) appear not only in the Westerns but in crime fiction in characters like Tali, the Israeli girl in *The Hunted,* or Luci Palma, the girl from the Dominican Republic in *Cat Chaser.*

Fenimore Cooper

Like Fenimore Cooper, whom Leonard as a child found verbose, he tangled from the start with the role of race in his stories. Eight of his fulllength Westerns feature men of color, and in all, Mexicans, Indians, or blacks play prominent roles. His most sympathetic characters tend to show an understanding of other cultures quite unusual in the Arizona of the time period. Sometimes this understanding is fostered by a residence among, or adoption by, the Apaches in Leatherstocking fashion, true in the case of Kirby Frye in *The Law at Randado* or John Russell in *Hombre.* Like Natty Bumppo, Roberto Valdez has battled Indians but has great respect for their ways, heightened because he has suffered the prejudice of Anglos. When he kills a black man in error, he seeks to indemnify the man's wife and to collect the wergild, the price of a man, from the bigoted and conscienceless Frank Tanner, who is responsible for the shooting.

Far and away the most dramatic of these men of color is John Russell, known like Natty Bumppo by a variety of names: Juan, or *tres hombres* to the Mexicans for a combat he undertook with three men, and Ishkay-Nay to the Apaches. As stoic as any Western hero, he may remind us of Fenimore Cooper's Uncas, who also dies in defense of a race for which he has no obligation to sacrifice his life.

Race

Even in these early books, however, Leonard tries to avoid creating paragons of virtue in his men of color, attempting to show many as fallible or worse. Such are a series of *segundos,* "seconds-in-command," nasty fellows like Phil Sundeen's Diego in *The Law at Randado,* or Emilio, Frank Tanner's in *Valdez Is Coming.* In later books with contemporary settings, Leonard has necessarily chosen more familiar figures, especially among his protagonists, many vaguely Irish American like himself, though some of mixed ancestry. But blacks and Hispanics continue to appear in large numbers, successfully treated as individuals rather than representatives. Any suggestion of patronizing flattery is so largely absent in Leonard's depictions, particularly of blacks—who may be good, bad, or indifferent—that he has been mistaken for being black himself on occasion by black readers.[1] He attributes this error waggishly to his first name, but it is a matter of no small personal satisfaction to him, and one that he feels flatters his writing talent.

The forceful, sympathetic figures of the Westerns, men of unflinching courage and remarkable physical prowess, had to be somewhat diminished in later fiction. Like Natty Bumppo, Paul Cable of *Last Stand at Saber River* outwits and outshoots his opponents, but Vince Mora of *Glitz*, three decades later, not only fails to shoot the heavy first—Linda Moon does the job—but takes Linda's bullet in his posterior as well.

Corey Bowen in *Escape from Five Shadows* often seems an amalgam of Gary Cooper and Natty Bumppo. Just as Cooper was attracted to Ingrid Bergman with her shorn head and gypsy connection in *For Whom the Bell Tolls*, so Bowen is attracted to Karla Demery: "Her short black hair making her look almost like a boy, yet strangely more feminine because of it. A slim body. Small even features. Clean-scrubbed, clean-smelling and dark from the sun, though you knew some of the warm brown was Mexican blood and you could see it in the eyes—one quarter from her mother's side."[2] Later, Bowen approaches the Mimbreno Apache Salvaje in one of those Fenimore Cooper–like parley scenes that Leonard resorts to both in Westerns and in crime fiction. Bowen puts himself totally in Indian hands, as Natty Bumppo does most dramatically in *The Deerslayer* when he, too, is a 20 year old. Salvaje holds Bowen "in high regard," remembering how he had offered superhuman resistance to the 10 warriors sent to return him to a convict camp from which he had escaped. Such heroics and such odds gradually diminish in later books, though Son Martin in *The Moonshine War* and Vincent Majestyk in *Mr. Majestyk* continue the tradition.

Anyone familiar with the genre knows that the Western requires walking a fine line between indulging the hackneyed and clichéd and working within an established tradition. Readers require a rousing narrative in which gunfights, holdups, jailbreaks, chases, and rescues are standard fare. Yet even such violent incidents may be treated originally—no quick draws on the main streets of dusty cow towns, for example. Leonard avoids sensational plotting. *The Law at Randado* features a particularly brutal lynching of Mexicans as well as a graphic whipping of the town's young marshal, but the complicity of the town's citizens in the lynching is handled realistically, as is the charitable treatment of the vicious Phil Sundeen (later to surface in *Gunsights*). Even the classic duello is given a new twist when the weapon used by Sundeen and the marshal proves to be not the six-shooter but the bottle. A decent fellow like Kirby Frye can hold his booze, and it is Sundeen who sinks beneath the tavern table to be carried ignominiously off to jail.

Documentation

In addition to maintaining that balance, the Western writer is faced with the problem of re-creating the life of a century ago, and Leonard is extraordinarily successful. He goes about the task of documenting his stories in as cold-blooded a fashion as he undertook the writing of Westerns, checking out whatever histories and memoirs of the Southwest he found in local libraries, drawing on Hollywood's best efforts, and making things up, for he has always believed as a writer and artist that the illusion of reality is more important than documentary realism. He has said with amused seriousness about his early books: "I subscribed to *Arizona Highways,* which gave me illustrations. If I needed a canyon, I'd go through the magazine, find one, and describe it."[3] This attention to detail and an uncanny sense of place are skills that Leonard discovered and honed in writing Westerns and would later bring to his crime fiction, to the pleasure of so many readers and moviegoers.

Leonard often jokes about his bloopers, for example, his discovery years ago that the mountains in Arizona looked nothing like the way he had described them. But his few mistakes and anachronisms pass largely unnoticed, just as they would later when he could afford extensive research. Most often in the Westerns, such lapses are limited to language. A character may say "dad" when the term "pa" was in general use, or in an egregious—and uncharacteristic—faux pas, Joe Medora, chief of scouts at Fort Bowie in the 1870s, resorts to a Yiddishism in a conversation with David Flynn, saying, "you bet your sweet tokus."[4] But these are carpings, since in the matters of weapons, horses, clothes, and scores of other things, Leonard is either right on the money or vague enough to escape notice.

As early as his first Western stories, Leonard enjoyed creating settings and backgrounds, confident that his imagination would assist him in making details real to his readers. In *Gunsights,* his last Western, he shows how effortlessly he can bring all the strands together in the depiction of someone like Bo Catlett, a black former cavalryman, the sort of man who must certainly have existed, as Leonard knew. But he adds a fresh mouth, a talent for playing the comic "darky" role when it suits him, and a knowledge of dynamite equaled only by Gary Cooper in *For Whom the Bell Tolls.*

Although in time he tired of Westerns, Leonard began enthusiastically, with the same enthusiasm he has today, for although he knows that writing is exhausting and demanding work, requiring enormous amounts of self-discipline, he enjoys it and often expresses delight that he is so well remunerated for having fun.

From the start, he wrote to meet the needs of a market, and there his copywriting experience stood him in good stead. You had to give the customer something more than the competition, he knew. Believing in your product helped, but so did packaging. The business required energy and long hours, but you had to conceal those efforts, always projecting enthusiasm and freshness.

Apprenticeship

The Westerns are the alembic from which he distilled the best for the later crime fiction—as difficult as that may be to comprehend for anyone who has read both (admittedly a small number). In the Westerns, Leonard began to learn to plot on a large scale and to unify his story as well as to pick up scores of tricks like starting fast, switching points of view, concealing a character's identity for a few paragraphs to catch a reader's attention, and using dialogue to advance the narration or even in place of narration. He purged his writing of adverbs, avoided metaphors and similes, began the habit of choosing the face or personality of a movie star like Gary Cooper or Harry Dean Stanton to serve as a model for a character, and learned to recycle material and to borrow from whatever was good and make it his own.

The biggest differences between his Westerns and later novels come in characterization, setting, and, most of all, humor. The superheroes who suffer endless indignities before lashing out in righteous indignation disappear. But a wonderful comic perception replaces them, an awareness not on the part of the dim bulbs who fill his pages—they never know they're funny—but on the part of Leonard himself. He creates a succession of lifelike figures whose foggy apprehension of moral norms is so aberrational, so totally off course, that they make us laugh despite ourselves. Such is Roy Hicks. Told that "a woman is beaten or physically abused something like every eighteen seconds," he replies: "You wouldn't think that many women get out of line, would you?"[5]

In the Westerns, however, Leonard relies on ironic situations or comic figures. The former are sometimes heavy-handed and mostly Hollywoodish, as when in *The Bounty Hunters,* the shavetail lieutenant Duane

Bowers, fresh out of West Point, successfully applies textbook Civil War strategy to defeat Apaches when he rallies Mexican *rurales* in a cavalry charge: "And there it was. Cavalry! Cavalry out of the Manual. Charging, full-glory cavalry used the way it should be, the way you dream about it but seldom see it. Something out of Cooke's *Tactics*" (*Bounty Hunters,* 176). In *Hombre* (1961), Leonard capitalizes on the ironic situation when John Russell decides good guys need not always handicap themselves by playing by the rules that the bad guys ignore.

Otherwise, humor is pretty much limited to breezy remarks between major figures, especially in the late effort *Gunsights,* or relegated to minor figures like Santana in *Bounty Hunters* who show a debt to the comic sidekicks of countless Western films. They in turn are the legacy of the comic servants of earlier literature, not to mention Fenimore Cooper's David Gamut, the comic Yankee psalmodist in *The Last of the Mohicans* and the precursor of any number of Eastern greenhorns, or the funny-looking partners of Gene Autry, Roy Rogers, and other heirs to Natty Bumppo.

Not until *Forty Lashes Less One,* Leonard's most eccentric Western and one of his oddest books, does a hint appear of what would be coming. *Forty Lashes* is set chiefly inside the Arizona Territorial Prison in Yuma in 1909 just before it closed, and while the novel contains sadistic guards and brutal beatings, familiar ingredients of *The Law at Randado, Escape from Five Shadows,* and *Gunsights,* the story is concerned less with Frank Shelby, a nasty convict who practically runs the prison, than with Raymond San Carlos and Harold Jackson. This unlikely but amusing twosome, one black, the other part Mexican and part Apache, have been imprisoned as a result of racial prejudice. Their escape comes about through the misguided notions of a ditzy new superintendent committed to reform. Everett Manly, a Holy Word Pentecostal preacher, encourages the skeptical San Carlos and Jackson to take pride in their racial heritages—as he understands them. The two, both American citizens, oblige him and make common cause as they begin practicing throwing homemade spears, painting their faces, and (most important to the plot) learning to run long distances without rest or water in a hostile landscape.

Sources and *The Bounty Hunters*

With the exception of *Forty Lashes,* Leonard's Western novels, like his pulp stories, are set in Apache Country, the area throughout Pima and

Cochise Counties, often near Fort Bowie and Apache Pass in Arizona. Leonard carefully read books available on Indian customs, such as John C. Cremony's classic *Life among the Apaches,* Frank C. Lockwood's *Apache Indians,* and J. Frank Dobie's volumes on the customs and history of the Southwest.[6] In addition, Leonard is influenced enormously by Hollywood films of the forties and fifties, such as *She Wore a Yellow Ribbon* (1949), starring John Wayne.

In 1952, shortly after selling "Cavalry Boots" for $100, Leonard published in *Dime Western* "You Never See Apaches," a title echoing the Bostonian Cremony's remark that "the Apache never shows himself, nor gives any sign of his presence."[7] Also in *Life among the Apaches,* Cremony, who served for a time with the United States Boundary Commission as an interpreter, recounts the rescue of two young Mexican captives from the Apaches. Cremony quotes an Apache leader asking for the return to a tribesman of the Mexican boys: "He has had one of these boys six years. He grew up under him. His heart-strings are bound around him. He is as a son to his old age. He speaks our language. . . . He loves the boy and cannot sell him" (Cremony, 65).

In *The Bounty Hunters,* Dave Flynn, who with Duane Bowers attempts to bring back the runaway Indian Soldado Viejo from Mexico to the San Carlos reservation, encounters what is apparently an Indian ambush of a Mexican family. But Flynn is not deceived for a moment. To him, as to Sherlock Holmes, "The signs were plain . . . because they were not there" (*Bounty Hunters,* 32). Seeing murdered children near the family's wagon, he knows the ambush could not have been carried out by the Indians: "They take the children . . . to bring them up in the tribe because there was always a shortage of men" (32).

Further, the very title of Leonard's book, *The Bounty Hunters,* as well as the incident of the ambush, may harken back to Cremony, who mentions one John Gallantin, an American reported to have accepted an offer from the Mexican governor of the state of Chihuahua of $30 for every Apache scalp he could provide and who was eventually "caught taking the scalps from the heads of several Mexicans murdered by his people in cold blood" (Cremony, 116). In *The Bounty Hunters,* Leonard assigns similar criminal activity to Curt Lazair, who actually stages the ambush so that it looks like the work of Indians.

Although Leonard's sources are not always identifiable, his sympathetic depiction of the Apache and of the passing of the Indian way of life is invariably in the Fenimore Cooper mode.[8] To be sure, young officers who must rescue a kidnapped woman, seasoned scouts, secret caves, noble chiefs, and stoic red men under torture, as well as references to the distinctive qualities of the Indian (what Cooper always calls "gifts"), have long since passed into public domain. Even Cremony, who regards the Apaches with disgust, finds himself forced to respect them as fighters and survivors true to their code, though he quickly assures his reader in the first chapter of *Life among the Apaches* that he has "considerably modified" those wrongheaded "impressions" of Fenimore Cooper.

Leonard's mood of melancholy resignation resembles Fenimore Cooper's when he portrays his Indians, magnificently adapted to their nomadic way of life, confronting the white man in an unequal contest they cannot hope to win. David Flynn can offer Soldado only an ill-planned agrarian alternative that spells a figurative, if not literal, death. Although he counsels the chief to return to subsistence farming on the San Carlos reservation, Flynn acknowledges in the spirit of *The Last of the Mohicans* that "the days of the Membrano [are] numbered . . . as well as the Chiricahua, Coyotero, Jicarilla and the Mescalero" (*Bounty Hunters,* 74). Neither white man nor Indian pretends that this outcome is anything less than a dispossession. Leonard's concern for the Indian ends, like Cooper's, in a refusal to distinguish between "bad" Indians and "good" but becomes a lament for all.

Dave Flynn, who never dodges a confrontation, prefigures Leonard heroes to come: a drifter, alienated but highly responsible in the Hemingway tradition, a man who, like Gary Cooper, acts only when pushed beyond endurance—but then, watch out! Like their cousins in the popular detective stories of the thirties, forties, and early fifties, the protagonists of these Westerns are "hard-boiled," dealing it out and taking it on a regular basis.

Although Paul Cable, Roberto Valdez, and John Russell are deadly with a Walker Colt or a Spencer Carbine, and capable of absorbing huge doses of physical punishment, they are also Ulysses-like, crafty men who combine cleverness and psychology with toughness. In decades to come, these early heroes would be transformed into guys like Harry Mitchell of *52 Pick-Up,* Cal Brown of *Swag,* and Chris Mankowski of *Freaky Deaky,* who sow distrust of each other among the bad guys, as Hawkeye does between the Mohawks and the Hurons. And in the fullness of time, they would become women like Kathy Diaz Baker of *Maximum Bob* and Karen Sisco of *Out of Sight,* who rely almost exclusively on their ability at psyching out the lowlifes.

In providing an elegy for the Indian within a hell-for-leather story of quick draws, face-offs, and captures, *The Bounty Hunters* supplies another ingredient that Leonard would use in the future: the popular uprising. In undisguised sympathy for the Mexican, either as victim of the Anglo or his own corrupt overlords, Leonard turns in a number of novels to episodes of popular revolt by the oppressed. First in *Bounty Hunters* under the leadership of Hilario Estaban, and also in *Joe Kidd* (1972), his first screenplay with Clint Eastwood, and in *Gunsights,* leaders arise to encourage their people to fight oppression. The tyrants range from Spanish troops in *Cuba Libre,* to grasping Anglo farm owners in *Mr. Majestyk,* or more ambiguously to United States Marines in the Dominican Republic in *Cat Chaser.* Some of these episodes seem faintly inspired by Hollywood films depicting the French Revolution or savor of efforts such as John Steinbeck's memorable script for *Viva Zapata* (1952).

When the finale of *The Bounty Hunters* comes, and the dust settles, the Apaches have been defeated. Sgt. Santana, one of those Leonard rascals who prove to contain as much good in them as bad, has become a better man, one who will try to be worthy of his country's glorious performance against France on the Cinco de Mayo at Puebla when Mexico defeated forces of Napoleon III. Assorted villains are dead—the less persistent reader might require a program to identify all the players—but the noble Soldado survives. As Oscar Wilde put it: "The good end happily, and the bad unhappily. That is what fiction means." The story is a rousing tribute to courage. It is both exciting and authentic, a good read.

The Law at Randado

The Law at Randado (1954) features the same Southwest settings Leonard had been using in his short stories, a boyish protagonist, and a similar cast of Mexicans, Apaches, and Anglos. But the plot relies heavily on a lynching incident, a topic that had been treated in American literature by William Faulkner, Thomas Wolfe, and Erskine Caldwell in the years between the two world wars and culminated in Walter Van Tilburg Clark's *The Ox-Box Incident* (1940), which Leonard had seen in its powerful film version during the war. Like Clark's novel, *Randado* is set in cattle country but focuses less on the collusion of the townspeople in the lynching than on a manhunt led by a young sheriff the town had expected to close his eyes. When Kirby Frye pursues Phil Sundeen, the bullying rancher behind the crime, Sundeen's men abandon him—with the exception of his hired gun Clay Jordan. Jordan is meant to be a menacing figure like the character played by Jack Palance in *Shane* the year before, but his disinterest in these events so closely approaches indifference that his comeuppance fails to stir the reader. "He died poorly," says Dandy Jim, a Coyotero Apache assisting Frye, echoing a similar remark made by Pablo in *For Whom the Bell Tolls*. Sundeen's ignominious though not fatal end at Kirby Frye's hand occasions a powerful lot of fence-mending in the community and Frye's reconciliation with Milmary Tindal, whose lack of faith in her beau hardly seems to earn her the gentle treatment she is accorded.

Escape from Five Shadows

Apparently aware of the unsatisfactory love interest he created in the prissy Milmary, Leonard sought inspiration from his ideal woman, Ingrid Bergman, in his next attempt, Karla Demery in *Escape from Five Shadows*. This book recounts the escape of Corey Bowen from a hellish prison camp named for nearby rock stratifications.

Unjustly accused of cattle theft (the Westerns seethe with the unjustly accused) Bowen has been seeking to escape from Frank Renda, who employs convict labor whom he exploits in construction projects. Bowen's escape depends on the cooperation of Karla Demery and the older, more worldly Lizann Falvey, wife of a besotted and intimidated government supervisor at the prison camp. Here Leonard borrows a device that Fenimore Cooper had borrowed from Sir Walter Scott, that of two enticing women, the one "pure," the other "tainted" by blood or sexual experience. To be sure, Edith Hanasian, no better than she should be, had flashed her dark eyes at Kirby Frye in *The Law at Randado,* but in *Five Shadows* the contrast is sharpened because Karla is a more attractive figure than Milmary, being self-reliant, heroic, and exuding a whiff of sex appeal absent in the other. Still, the love interest fails to ignite. Lizann Falvey, Karla's competition, awakens little more than pity as the weary victim of two despicable males, her husband and Frank Renda; and the novel concludes with Karla and Corey vaguely intending to see more of each other, an ending not much different than that of *Randado.*

Last Stand at Saber River

Last Stand at Saber River (1959) is conventional but conventionally satisfying as well. It features one of Leonard's few domesticated protagonists, Paul Cable, and shows earmarks of *Shane,* which Leonard had greatly relished (except for Alan Ladd's diminutive hat, which he felt might bet-

ter have belonged to Dale Evans, Roy Rogers's resolute helpmeet).
Cable is a paterfamilias, a recently returned Confederate veteran whose
sudden appearance suggests nearly mythic origins. A clever, resolute,
and courageous soldier determined to reclaim his usurped property and
reestablish his family, he could almost be Ulysses. More likely, however,
he is just another of those *Blut und Boden* homesteaders featured in
movies like *Shane* or *3:10 to Yuma* who find themselves up against powerful ranchers. As might be expected, his battle against a duo of ruthless
men and their hirelings determined to eradicate him offers few surprises.
But it does offer a few.

Once again, the hands of Hemingway and probably Fenimore
Cooper as well appear, but to a lesser extent than in other novels. The
two women are back, but this time the boyish one, Lorraine Kidston, (a
teenage seductress with too much time on her hands) tests the virtue of
Paul Cable, and the older one, his wife, like Penelope, never falters in
her trust and devotion. The Hemingway touches appear largely in the
landscapes and the single protagonist who could be Robert Jordan:
"Paul Cable sat hunched forward at the edge of the pine shade, his boots
crossed and his elbows supported on his knees. He put the field glasses
to his eyes again and, four hundred yards down the slope, the two story
adobe was brought suddenly, silently before him."[9]

This description closely follows the opening sentences of *For Whom the
Bell Tolls,* as does the view below with its Spanish flavor and the girl who
soon appears, Luz Acaso. But it is just as likely that the movies influenced scenes like this as much as Hemingway (or even Fenimore Cooper
with his debt to the Hudson River school painters), since after the
advent of Technicolor, such panoramic shots became a staple of the
Westerns.

In any event, the reader, like the filmgoer, watches from above the
silent scene below, uneasily aware that what appears static—like a
painted landscape—will not remain so long. And when the Mexican girl
comes out of the adobe, the reader wonders what effect she and the
inhabitants of the adobe will have on the lives of the observers. Even
from above in the trees, Paul and his wife, Martha, can discern that Luz
looks "tired or ill," and when a male figure steps out of the house, the
chill perceptibly grows: "He was a tall man, heavy boned, somewhat thin
with dark hair and mustache. He was perhaps in his late thirties. His left
arm was off between the shoulder and the elbow" (*Last Stand*, 3).

In typical Western fashion, the protagonist battles against heavy
odds. Paul Cable defeats superior forces using skills he had developed

both in the war and in his encounters with the Apaches. Although he is mauled and insulted, he triumphs. At the end, the stage is littered with corpses, but Paul Cable and Vern Kidston, one of his chief adversaries, discover a mutual liking as they realize how both have been victimized by Edward Janroe, a former Confederate officer and unreconstructed fanatic. Janroe is revealed to be a traitor to all and to possess the mentality of the treacherous Pablo of *For Whom the Bell Tolls* and the grandiose delusions of Fenimore Cooper's Lieutenant Muir of *The Pathfinder*.

Hombre

Hombre, Leonard tells us, "was finished in 1959 and rejected by publishers for nearly two years before Ballantine bought it for $1,250" (Geherin, 8). He completed the book at the peak of America's Western craze in a year when more than two dozen of them clogged prime-time television, and the bonanza was about to end. Indeed, the sum he got, as David Geherin noted, was "barely more than he had earned for his first story in 1951" ["Trail of the Apache," in *Argosy*] (8).

Hombre, like *Escape from Five Shadows, Last Stand at Saber River,* and *Valdez Is Coming,* features a single, almost entirely self-reliant protagonist who contends in epic style against multiple enemies. Such stories are what many readers associate with the classic Western and what Leonard relied on in his most stylized and traditional tales. Although he would never abandon the notion of one man against many, vital as well in his crime fiction, he would come to make concessions in stories in which the complexities of life require more interaction than novels like *Hombre* would seem to suggest. For all the man-against-the-sky quality of *Hombre* and his insistence that it is a first-person narration, Leonard's story does not convey the immediacy that such a point of view suggests. Rather, the story is told by Carl Everett Allen, a minor figure, one of the passengers aboard a "mud wagon," a light coach used in springtime when roads may be soft. Allen figures very slightly in the story, revealing himself only when he is romantically musing about "the McLaren girl," a 17 year old who had been four weeks an Apache prisoner.

In *Hombre*, the spotlight is on John Russell, a man of mixed blood, and the "two women" theme barely surfaces. The vixen, the wife of a crooked Indian agent, is as shady as her husband. Her foil, called only "the McLaren girl," is so faintly sketched that Hollywood found it necessary to replace her in the Paul Newman movie (*Hombre,* 1967) with a flashier favorite, the saloon floozy who brightened *Stagecoach* and TV's *Gunsmoke*. This stock character, a version of the "hooker with the heart of gold," goes back at least to Dumas, and Leonard would certainly have been wary of her.

The hombre, John Russell, reluctantly accepts the role of protector of a mixed bag of passengers threatened by robbers, though they show little but prejudice and contempt for his swarthy hue and suspicious origins. The villains are out to get a sum of money, as they usually are in Leonard's novels. In this case, it has been stolen from Apaches by Dr. Alexander Favor, formerly of the San Carlos reservation and a slippery evangelical clergyman who had been appointed agent there in accordance with the policy of the Bureau of Indian Affairs. Dissimilar people thrown together by chance had not only worked in *Stagecoach* but went back as far as *Grand Hotel* (1932) and *Lifeboat* (1944), and Leonard makes the formula work again by introducing a few new wrinkles. That he is not above borrowing a trick or two, though, is evident in the scene when John Russell unhurriedly digs his Spencer rifle out of the baggage after a stagecoach holdup and coolly picks off Lamar Dean as he rides off with Favor's $12,000. Variations of that scenario have graced any number of movies, but it always works. Naturally, Lamar Dean richly deserved his fate, and in addition he proved his stupidity by not recognizing Russell, with whom he had had an earlier run-in. Leonard has very little patience with dolts, especially arrogant ones.

Eventually Russell is able to guide the band to a hillside assay shack, where the outlaws, still after that $12,000, discover them. A parley between the groups ensues. Leonard claims that this scene, mentally envisioned, was the genesis of the whole book; and still today he visualizes a brief scene with dialogue as it might appear on a movie screen and then constructs his book by explaining what led up to this event and what follows.

Parleys figure in most Westerns and are a device Fenimore Cooper was particularly fond of, too. What bothers Leonard in *Hombre*, however, is that in negotiations conducted under a flag of truce, honorable men invariably practice fair play, but outlaws always cheat. Thirty years later, Leonard described the scene he wrote for *Hombre* this way:

> The lead heavy mounts the hill with a white hanky hanging from his Winchester, stands outside the shack and states his terms. Give him the money in exchange for water and chuck and everybody goes home. The spokesman for the good guys says they'll have to think it over. The lead heavy tells them to be sure of one thing: they're not leaving here with the

money. As he turns to go another one of the good guys says, "I got a
question. . . . How you going to get down that hill?"[10]

The answer to that query provides not only a host of ethical questions
but solid action as well. And the sum of money? It would stand Leonard
in good stead for dozens of novels.

Russell dies soon afterward, shot by a nameless Mexican. His sacrificial death is largely ignored by the others, though the McLaren girl will
see that a mass is said for the repose of his soul, and Carl Everett Allen
speaks a eulogy proper for an epic hero: "You will never see another one
like him as long as you live" (*Hombre*, 190).

In future books, Leonard remained cautious about killing off major
sympathetic figures. He did it again with Angela Nolan, murdered by
Robbie Daniels in *Split Images,* and Gary Hammond, shot to death by
Elvin Crowe in *Maximum Bob*. Both of these deaths were risky ventures
for popular fiction, since they neither come at the end nor appear to be
of great meaning. By contrast, the reader is prepared for the death of
John Russell and accepts it with regret as meaningful.

Valdez Is Coming

After *The Big Bounce* (1969), Leonard "tagged up" again, turning back
to another Western, *Valdez Is Coming*, his sixth full-length effort at the
genre. Inspiration came from two short stories about a character named
Bobby Valdez, but the idea of a Mexican American lawman goes back at
least to "The Hard Way" (*Zane Grey's Western,* August 1953), in which a
deputy sheriff of Hispanic origin named Jimmy Robles comes up against
Anglo prejudice. In 1954 Leonard published a story about the hanging
of 22-year-old Bobby Valdez called "Saint with a Sixgun" (*Argosy,* October 1954). Then, seven years later, he recycled his older material and
brought back Bobby Valdez, now a few years younger, just as Fenimore
Cooper had done with Natty Bumppo. For *Valdez Is Coming* Leonard
began with the same episode he used in "Only Good Ones" (*Western
Writers of America Anthology Roundup,* 1961), even keeping some of the
characters' names but making the resurrected Valdez older by a score or
more of years.

Valdez dramatizes a single figure who must right a wrong and who
becomes in the course of the story an avenging demigod of the sort that
continues through to Sylvester Stallone's *Rambo* films. The novel often
draws on Hemingway's prose rhythms, sometimes to a point of pas-
tiche: "Luck was all right when you had it, but it couldn't be counted

on. It worked good and bad, but it worked more good than bad if you knew what you were doing."[11] Derivative, too, is the device of the man of two identities, the one mild mannered, the other deadly and danger-ous. Bobby Valdez changes from the self-effacing public servant of early pages to Roberto Valdez, the man of few words, as silent and as quick as the rattlesnake or the Apache with whom he shares the mountains and the canyons. Pop sources such as the comics and the pulps had enshrined the device of the double identity in the persons of the Green Hornet, Superman, and Batman and Robin, though it had actually come into favor earlier via the Baroness Orczy's *Scarlet Pimpernel* (1905). Roberto Valdez's transition is not as melodramatic as that of comic book figures, but like those superheroes, he shuns his town dress for his old Apache-fighting outfit to become "the Valdez from another time, the Valdez in leather chivara pants and the long-barreled Walker Colt on his right thigh carrying his shotgun and a Sharps carbine and field glasses and a big canteen and a warbag for the ham and biscuits, the Valdez no one had seen in ten years" (*Valdez*, 92).

Slow to anger but implacable in his wrath, this heir of the conquista-dors takes on Frank Tanner, a conventional Leonard villain, and his army of retainers, because Tanner refuses to compensate the pregnant Indian wife of a black settler inadvertently shot by Valdez in circumstances cre-ated by Tanner. In a series of encounters, he destroys as many enemies as any hero of sagas and, before the final scene, succeeds in winning Tan-ner's woman, who combines the roles of both the woman with a past and the virtuous woman. The love scene is pure Hemingway. Gay explains, like Maria of *For Whom the Bell Tolls,* that she has no family, nowhere to go; and then, underneath the sky (as in the sleeping bag episode), she asks:

> "Where should I spread my blanket?"
> "Where do you want to?"
> Looking down at him she said, "Wherever you tell me." (*Valdez*, 132)

Forty Lashes Less One

Forty Lashes Less One, written before *Valdez,* marks a clearer change toward Leonard's crime fiction than the later novel because it rejects the notion of utterly self-reliant, steely heroes and concerns itself more with the interaction of fallible characters while achieving a certain level of comedy amid the usual villainy and misdeeds. *Valdez,* on the other hand, despite its starker form, produces a final calm of passions spent that rejects violence and noble savagery for noble civilization—not to mention domesticity, since Valdez will return to the law and to the town, maybe even with Gay. Thus *Forty Lashes* falls somewhere between *The Bounty Hunters* and *Gunsights,* for the former concludes in a hail of gunfire and a cavalry charge whereas the latter ends in combat deferred as reporters and onlookers surge forward, aware they are watching history in the making, but recognizing the conclusory nature of it as well.

Gunsights

Gunsights is Leonard's last Western, though not his last Western story or screenplay. As such, it might be considered his farewell to the genre, since like Prospero in *The Tempest,* he puts aside his book of magic after this to concentrate on crime fiction. A more apt comparison is with Fenimore Cooper, who in *The Prairie* (1827) kills off an aged Natty Bumppo, no longer a lethal Indian fighter and scout but a humble trapper and an anachronism. *Gunsights* sounds a similar elegiac note, though with a smiling acknowledgment that the sort of charming immaturity of the West, the Western, and the book's dual protagonists is ready to accede to more grownup ways.

The clearest artistic debts of *Gunsights* are to *High Noon* (1952), *Butch Cassidy and the Sundance Kid* (1969), and Leonard's own *Bounty Hunters,* with its oblique allusions to Fenimore Cooper, including again the two women—competitors of sorts, one more morally compromised than the other.

Brendan Early and Dana Moon (who greatly resemble Dave Flynn and Duane Bowers of *The Bounty Hunters,* right down to the Colt .44 packed in a shoulder rig that both Moon and Flynn wear) had ridden into Mexico a half-dozen years before the story opens (just as Flynn and Bowers had) to return some Indians who had jumped the reservation. This time it is Loco and his braves who also managed to kidnap the redoubtable Katherine McKean. In place of Curt Lazair and his bloodthirsty bounty hunters are Phil Sundeen and his. Although Sundeen first appeared in *The Law at Randado,* there is little but his old meanness and arrogance to connect the two roles.

A portion of the story is concerned with Early and Moon's conflict with Sundeen, who is also hunting Loco, and culminates in a shoot-out, the so-called Sonora Incident, when Sundeen appears to be killed. More concerns Sundeen's vendetta against the two in later years, coming to a head when he becomes the hireling of a mining company determined to run settlers off lands deemed mineral rich.

Taking place in the copper country of Arizona in the late 1880s and early 1890s, *Gunsights* is narrated with great confidence, allowing Leonard to juggle flashbacks and flash-forwards without difficulty and to vary scenes from parlors to hillsides, from courtrooms to jails and mining offices. In addition, he makes use of a figure who is not exactly a "central intelligence" (he is too naive and peripheral) but provides the critical perspective of an outsider.

Toward the climax of the book, LaSalle Mining, under the pragmatic leadership of a Mr. Vandozen from New Jersey, is growing disenchanted with Phil Sundeen, the head of the company's Security Division. He has engaged a motley crew of "saddle bums and gunnysackers" attracted by posters promising "HIGH PAY" and "INTERESTING WORK." But LaSalle is now ready to make a deal with Dana Moon; eager, in fact, since it has been recently learned that the Rincon Mountains, where the troublesome settlers dwell, contain only meager amounts of copper ore.

Brendan Early, entrusted to convey this intelligence to his on-again, off-again companion Dana Moon (their crusty impatience with each other is a *Butch Cassidy*–like note), prefers instead to egg on Phil Sundeen into one last fight. In Tom Sawyer fashion, Early, who has never quite grown up, urges the bully to avenge his humiliation at Sonora years before, telling him he has an opportunity "to get your name in the history books."[12]

In *Gunsights* people of color defend their land against a white enemy whose brutality and technology are restrained only by fear of the press with its access to the place of conflict. This situation suggests that news coverage of the recently concluded Vietnam War was still fresh in Leonard's mind. The struggle between ragtag Indians, Mexicans, and mixed-blood elements against Sundeen's mercenary force is covered by a large group of cynical reporters who make their headquarters in hotels and bars while they cover the "Rincon Mountain War" or the "Last of the Great Indian Nigger Wars" (*Gunsights,* 7). They wait for word that will send them rushing into the field just as reporters waited in Saigon hotels and bars or collected afternoons for the "Five O'Clock Follies," the daily statement issued by the United States Army.[13]

The presence of photographers and of Colonel Billy Washington (a Buffalo Bill clone), eager to sign up Early and Moon to tour with his Wild West Show, proves so disconcerting to Sundeen's army of thugs that they desert. Sundeen is obliged to advance alone toward the small party of opposition waiting beside the house that Dana Moon (now married to Kate McKean) shares. Distracted by the confusion of the event, Moon is a tad slower than usual in his lightning response to Sundeen's shouted challenge. But Sundeen's speed with his gun is not fast enough, either, for Kate has already blasted him with a Henry rifle even before her husband begins to fire. As husband and wife pour slugs into the scoundrel, Brendan Early comes running, but he is too late. "Too late" is the leitmotiv for this novel: too late for melodrama, too late for the West, and too late for the Western. Adventure and derring-do of this sort are finished. The Mimbre Apaches return to their desolate farms, and Sundeen's desperadoes ostensibly look for new work. With resignation touched with admiration, Kate tells Moon and Early, who are now considering Colonel Billy Washington's offer to join his Wild West Show, that they themselves are the show.

The Comedy Is Ended

Although Leonard is often ambiguous in his treatment of women in early books, here Kate serves as his *raisonneur,* demonstrating how far Leonard has come from figures such as Nita Estaban of *The Bounty Hunters,* an abused female who lives for a time in a cave as a servant to her captors and whose characterization is greatly indebted to the submissive Maria of *For Whom the Bell Tolls.* Perhaps *Gunsights* marks a farewell to Gary Cooper, too, since the novel dimisses not only the Ingrid Bergman figure but the entirety of Hemingway's weltschmerz as well. Like "The Bride Comes to Yellow Sky," *Gunsights* celebrates the end of an era and a new life of maturity and responsibility. As for Fenimore Cooper, *Gunsights* is the last novel in which the true ownership of the land—Cooper's great theme in *The Leatherstocking Tales*—plays a prominent role. After this book, Leonard concentrates on milieus where the only land is "turf."

Chapter Three

Up in Michigan

The work of a prolific writer like Leonard might be classified in several ways; by chronology and genre seemed appropriate for the Westerns. But it is not for those short stories and books that Leonard is now read or will be remembered, and his later novels are not all of a piece. To find a common denominator, it is convenient to consider them according to their settings, since readers admire Leonard's books for their strong sense of place. This fact is all the more significant if we consider that he is far less concerned with detailed descriptions, particularly of interiors or even weather, than we might expect of a writer for whom the insides of houses and the extremes of American climate are important. Thus though he largely ignores particulars that might be expected, he has succeeded from the days when he set stories in the Dragoon Mountains of eastern Arizona to the late nineties with his Detroit and Miami locales (not to mention Cuba or Hollywood) in conveying an unmistakable contemporary scene.

One hallmark of his recent fiction has been the implicit comparison and contrast of North and South as personified by southern Florida (Miami and its environs) and Detroit (together with Oakland County and the shore of Lake Huron). Inside these perimeters, marginal white Americans move uneasily among blacks and Hispanics in a country where crime has become just another business. Leonard is most concerned with decayed downtowns, but he often transports his characters out into the suburbs as well. His Detroit, for example, is a place of rubble-strewn lots and boarded-up storefronts where a chastened auto industry has moved to the suburbs, still a mighty force, but one that has lost a third of the domestic market. Detroit's touted Renaissance Center, a frequent locale, towers ironically over a moribund city, and when a couple of ambitious holdup men like Frank Ryan and Ernest Stickley go into business, they head north of Seven Mile Road to places like Leonard's own neighborhood where the houses often have million-dollar-plus price tags.

In similar fashion, Miami Beach is seen both as a symbol of glitz, the sort of place where Gianni Versace restored a villa, and as the down-at-

the-heels haunt of elderly retired Jews from New York, Marielitos
dumped by Castro, and "good old boys" drifted down from the Panhan-
dle, all cautiously circling each other in a simmering brew. As Michael
Wood said in the *Times Literary Supplement,* "the old locations, Los Angeles and New York, seem tame and faded, almost genteel. The real meanness is on the streets of Detroit, Miami. . . ."[1] And it is chiefly on these
streets that Leonard plays out his complicated dramas of betrayal and
dysfunction with a large, memorable cast of characters who work their
scams speaking American English, and whose sagas, as one book critic
after another insists, are "impossible to put down."

The "First" Book

The Big Bounce, Leonard's first novel to move away from a Western setting, is a transitional work measured by any standard. The book displays
a number of weaknesses, most of which proved instructive, since he
overcame them inside five years. Revised piecemeal several times as he
sought to interest publishers in a manuscript he claims was rejected 84
times, the book suffers from an inconsistency of tone. From the hindsight of his numerous triumphs, it is hard to see now how his canny
agent H. N. Swanson could have waxed enthusiastic about this new
property. But wax he did, and his optimism ("I'm going to make you
rich") infected Leonard, boosting his confidence at what was a critical
juncture, a step in a new direction, for although he would return to
Westerns again briefly, *The Big Bounce* marks the start of Elmore
Leonard's career as a significant American writer.

The protagonist of the book, Jack Ryan, is an Irish Catholic from
Detroit who has gotten a ride back to Michigan from the Southwest
with migrant Mexican laborers, and he has temporarily thrown his lot in
with them. Leonard knew next to nothing about Mexican *braceros,* but
he had seen the shacks they lived in, and their appearance during the
summer so far north had piqued his interest. Five years later, having
read informally a good deal about Cesar Chavez's attempt to organize
such workers, he would treat them again in Arizona in *Mr. Majestyk,*
borrowing the name of a character from *The Big Bounce* for the new
effort, though not the character himself.

Jack Ryan, the sort of tough, stand-up guy who had appeared in
Leonard's novels before and would continue to, becomes involved with
Nancy Hayes, a psychotic teenage bimbo whose very existence often
puts Jack in an unfavorable light. Like so many of Leonard's men with a

past, Jack's faint aura of danger seems to make him attractive to women, and two vie for his favors, though nothing really works out. Nancy Hayes reveals herself to him in time as so perfidious and unstable as to be not worth his bother, and Virginia Murray's role becomes little more than a walk-on.

When he leaves the migrant camp after a brouhaha with the Mexican crew leader, Luis Camacho, Jack finds employment with Walter Majestyk, a crusty old justice of the peace and motel owner. At his lakeside motel, not too different from the one Leonard's mother owned in Pompano Beach, Jack is briefly involved with Virginia Murray, a guest. When he is about to seduce her, the young woman blurts out that she's Catholic, and he replies, "So am I."[2] Doubtful, she challenges him to recite the Apostles' Creed. His ability to do so puts a damper on the moment for both in a scene where Leonard's uncertain handling of passion and intimacy is saved by something like the comic touch that is a feature of his books from the next decade on.

The greatest weakness of *The Big Bounce* is its tendency to come perilously close to soap opera. Leonard attempts to remedy the situation by backing off from the melodramatic. Thus Jack and Virginia zipper themselves up and take leave of a scene that would have required more development of the relationship between the two or risked showing Jack as even more irresponsible than he appears. A more significant episode is Jack's rejection of Nancy Hayes's scheme to steal the $50,000 payroll of the migrant workers—for what reason we are never sure: is it because he realizes that the teenage temptress is exploiting him, or because he has moral stirrings, or because he simply sees that he would be a prime suspect in any police investigation?

The Big Bounce recounts the story of a young man with a past (mostly housebreaking) who becomes acquainted with a girl looking for a special thrill, "the big bounce." Nancy Hayes is the sort of jailbait teenager that Erskine Caldwell wrote about in the sixties, specializing in voyeuristic behavior and destructive rampages in the houses where she baby-sits before seducing her young charges' fathers. Then, out of pure meanness, she sends letters to the wives of the men with whom she has dallied, saying they have been "seen taking advantage of a sixteen-year-old girl" (*Big Bounce,* 36). One of her most willing victims, wealthy Ray Ritchie of Ritchie Foods, takes her back from her posh Gold Coast Florida home to Michigan, where he installs her in his lakeside hunting lodge.

Before Jack's arrival, Nancy—out of sheer boredom—has been working her charms on Bob Rogers Jr., Ritchie's majordomo. Bob's hatred of Jack both as a rival for Nancy and as a troublemaker in the migrant camp promises to provide *Bounce* with a certain amount of suspense until Leonard becomes aware that morally and ethically there is precious little difference between the two men. The result is a bloody fight between them, after which the two sled dogs shake hands and make up. But Bob Rogers's transformation from a sneering bully to a regular fellow comes too quickly to be credible, even though this kind of change in character occurs less awkwardly in novels before and after *Bounce*.

When they are together, Jack and Nancy sneak about in the dark breaking windows of houses in the resort community, once even firing a Colt Woodsman .22 at several inappropriate targets. Long passages devoted to the delights of prowling through houses when people are out—or even better, not out—give the novel a morbid tone. The sympathy generated for Jack is constantly dissipated by his collusion with Nancy in her nocturnal raids. Nancy is portrayed not as a wild young thing but as a snotty sicko. Leonard, however, is indecisive in her depiction, betraying a kind of awe at her contempt of lower-class interior decorating. At one point, she compares the blue-collar families spending a week on Lake Huron to dazzled Russian workers awarded vacations at Black Sea resorts, as if this unintellectual teenager were a reader of *Soviet Life* or a student of Eastern Europe.[3] Although Nancy's connoisseurship of wines extends only as far as cold duck, both the proletarian Jack and the author seem impressed. Indeed, in a waterside story containing many faint echoes of *The Great Gatsby,* Nancy becomes a kind of cut-rate version of Fitzgerald's Daisy Buchanan, right down to the fact that both women carelessly hit pedestrians with cars.

In *The Big Bounce,* Leonard talks too much in his own voice while pretending to convey the thoughts of his characters, a mistake he doesn't make again. As he progressed, he learned to cut out anything that "looks like writing" and let the dialogue take over much of the job of advancing the narration:

> The idea had come to her suddenly right after seeing him at the migrant camp. The idea was wild, so far out she had only smiled at first, thinking of what it would do to Ray Ritchie. But the more she thought of the idea, the more she liked it. It was fantastic, way out, and beyond anything she had ever done before. The trouble was, the whole thing would depend on Ryan. It would depend first on whether or not he was staying around Geneva Beach instead of going home, and second, it would depend on his nerve. (*Big Bounce,* 44)

In this passage—not yet the work of a "Panasonic ear"—Nancy's plan is
dangled before us in a provocative fashion. Clearly it involves taking
revenge on Ray Ritchie, who, she feels, has wronged her; and just as
clearly we are going to have to wait to find out what "the idea" is,
though we are allowed to know it is "wild," "far out," even "way out."
Her obvious delight alerts us to wickedness afoot. All that is missing in
the mental soliloquy is maniacal laughter. Leonard justifiably prides
himself that his characters tell the story, that what we hear is only their
words and thoughts, but here authorial intrusion is evident.

Much later in the novel, Jack points out to Nancy the field hands'
camp beyond the cucumber fields and starts an introspective little talk
on the essential happiness of their simple lives, concluding that "they
still have something not many people have." She replies sarcastically
first that this "something" must be "dignity." The pretentious tone vanishes when Jack says, "go bag your ass," more likely how Leonard himself was feeling about the direction the scene was taking (*Big Bounce*,
153). The humor is a welcome relief in a glum book, and a favorable
prognostication, for Leonard's gift for humor would soon loom.

52 Pick-Up

Although Leonard doesn't return to a Michigan setting for five more
books, in many respects he picks up where he left off. Again he turns to
the subject of an older man involved with a teenage mistress; but it is
Harry Mitchell who is the focus of *52 Pick-Up*, not Cini Fisher, a nude
model who has been set up in comfortable circumstances by her lover in
Detroit. Harry is depicted sympathetically. Unlike Ray Ritchie, Harry is
no lecherous philanderer, but a self-made entrepreneur of working-class
origins who has made it into the most expensive suburbs. Approaching
his fifties, Harry, an amalgam of Ray Ritchie and Jack Ryan (and probably Leonard, whose own marriage had begun to falter), is undergoing a
familiar midlife crisis.

When a trio of blackmailers demand a whopping sum to keep his
secret, Harry manfully confesses to his wife, Barbara, and determines to
fight them. In a consequent retrospective of their marriage from Barbara's point of view, Leonard demonstrates how skillfully he has over-
come the problems he faced only five years before when entering the
mind of Nancy Hayes, perhaps because Barbara's thoughts might just
as easily have been those of a man as she sadly pores over old photo
albums: "There were pictures taken at a party at least eighteen or

twenty years ago. Look at how young everyone looked. Good friends who were still friends, most of them. Everyone laughing."[4]

In every respect, *52 Pick-Up* surpasses *The Big Bounce*. The "caper" that fizzled in *Bounce* works here as Harry takes on three criminals single-handedly in the style of Western heroes John Russell or Roberto Valdez. The level of violence increases when the blackmailers force Harry to witness a "snuff" film of Cini being murdered in a chair with Harry's own gun. Leonard calls his Detroit stories urban Westerns facetiously, and *52 Pick-Up* qualifies in most respects. As self-reliant as Roberto Valdez in pursuing the thugs who mean to pursue him, Harry turns them against each other and destroys them singly, the last with the dynamite that figures so prominently in the Arizona stories (and *For Whom the Bell Tolls*). For *52 Pick-Up,* Leonard brings together successfully for the first time all the strands of the typical Leonard thriller: the "caper" that provides the title, a payoff of $52,000 to be delivered as ransom for Barbara; a subplot involving an opportunist's attempt to capitalize on Harry and Barbara's marital discord; humor, violence, and slick detective work on Harry's part, whose rules of life (the Hemingway touch again) help him to cut through the machinations of the dysfunctional lowlifes who betray themselves and others in the sleazy world of the inner-city porn business. Finally, the novel concludes with a plot twist as a villain is caught in his own trap.

Frank and Ernest: *Swag*

Leonard felt so comfortable with the ingredients of *52 Pick-Up* that he turned to many of them for *Swag,* especially the familiar locales. As a former auto assembly line worker, now the owner of a machine and tool plant with yearly gross sales of close to $3 million, Harry Mitchell moved credibly between Detroit's upscale suburbs and the milieu that spawned his antagonists—the bars, "adult" movie theaters, and storefront studios for the photography of naked models. Again in *Swag,* Leonard not so much contrasts a ravaged Detroit with the townships above Fourteen Mile Road (including his own Bloomfield Hills, where Harry lives) as compares them in the same way he shows a sun-drenched Florida not so different from a chilly Detroit.

As he had often done before, he switched from a single protagonist to a duo. In a playful fashion, he named them Frank and Ernest, Frank Ryan and Ernest Stickley, but deliberately made nothing of the names.[5] The importance of being Ernest, however, becomes apparent as his role grows at Frank's expense, and he turns up in *Stick* some seven years later.

Swag relates the misadventures of two engaging stickup men who meet in circumstances Leonard used again in *Killshot*. Frank Ryan realizes that Ernest Stickley is the man he's been looking for to embark on a career of armed robbery. As a result, Frank refuses to identify Ernest at a pretrial examination as the man whom he had earlier fingered for stealing a maroon '73 Camaro from the Chevrolet agency where he works.

The enterprise, Frank assures Stick, cannot fail, provided they both adhere to a set of rules. Here Leonard gently parodies the code heroes of so many of his earlier books, straight-shooting, fair men, true to themselves. Ryan's rules—actually the original hardcover title of *Swag*—rather than being a moral code, a Ten Commandments written for Stick by Ryan on "ten different cocktail napkins," are more a list of dos and don'ts, in part cautionary ("# 3 NEVER CALL YOUR PARTNER BY NAME—UNLESS YOU USE A MADE-UP NAME"), in part stressing etiquette ("# 1 ALWAYS BE POLITE ON THE JOB, SAY PLEASE AND THANK YOU") (*Swag,* 17). In lending a certain cavalier quality to his duo, Leonard puts them to some extent in the ancient tradition of gentleman bandits. Their failure to observe rule 10, "NEVER ASSOCIATE WITH PEOPLE KNOWN TO BE IN CRIME," brings disaster to them (17).

The relationship between Frank and Stick is depicted as marriagelike. (In 1979 Leonard would tread the same ground again in *Gunsights,* where the debt to *Butch Cassidy and the Sundance Kid* is more apparent.) Frank is the talky Detroiter, full of himself, formerly a car salesman at Red Bowers Chevrolet; Stick is the down-home country boy, originally from Oklahoma, shrewd and commonsensical—or at least as shrewd and commonsensical as a stickup man is likely to be—and Leonard's favorite. In the four months they are together, they often get on each other's nerves, and only a commitment to the business arrangement they have keeps them going. Living in Villa Monterey, their new apartment in Troy (a developing suburb about 15 miles from downtown Detroit), "a cream-colored stucco building with . . . a Spanish tile roof . . . and swimming pool," plunges them head-on into the seventies singles scene (*Swag,* 41). Their involvement with the "career ladies" of Villa Monterey requires more graphic sexual depiction than Leonard had hitherto written, though it is rarely detailed and sometimes ends in failure—for instance, Stick's coitus interruptus when Arlene flees him, called to a modeling session for Hi Performance Cams. Arlene's return at the end of the novel is crucial to the wry twist that concludes it,

whereas other anecdotes are casually gratuitous, like that of Mona—
nomen est omen—the prostitute whose audible lovemaking titillates the
building's residents.

A mixture of comedy and gripping suspense, the armed robberies in
liquor stores, gas stations, and supermarkets the duo pulls in the suburbs north and west of Detroit serve as an exciting curtain-raiser for the
big caper, the holdup of the J. L. Hudson Company, which occupies the
second half of the book. Frank and Stick allow themselves to be per-
suaded by Sportree, the black owner of the Royal Lounge on West Eight
Mile Road, to participate in the holdup of a big downtown department
store. An old friend of Frank's, Sportree had previously tipped them off
as to where they could steal some "clean" guns and has devised a scheme
to steal a bundle at no risk to himself.

Plans are hatched in Sportree's apartment above the bar, a typical
Leonard hideout, a Gothic vestige traceable to the pulps he devoured
years earlier, where provocative women slunk about as the skulduggery
developed. Although it contains no sliding panels or secret doors—
another pulp favorite, resuscitated for *City Primeval*—the lounge is
patronized in the hours after work by whites and by an entirely black
clientele at night, showing that evil is an equal-opportunity employer.
Leonard's touch in all this is light as Sportree and his henchman Leon
Woody explain to the white boys how they will burst into the credit
department at Hudson's at just the time Brinks makes its regular collection. Bags of cash identified by Sportree's inside contact, the sexy
Marlys, will be hidden inside a doll's cardboard box, to be stashed until
pickup later in the toy department's storeroom:

> "Little Curly Laurie Walker's box," Leon Woody said.
> Sportree began to smile and shook his head.
> "Come on, shit—Curly Laurie Walker. That her name?"
> "Little redhead girl, three foot tall, she do everything but bleed," Leon
> Woody said. (*Swag,* 169)

Stick's increasing doubts about these black men, "relying on . . . people he didn't even know" (*Swag,* 148), prove justified when the holdup
results in two killings, and Sportree and Leon Woody betray Frank and
Stick, keeping the money. Moreover, the cops are hot on Stick's trail and
ambush him when he goes to Hudson's to retrieve the doll's box.
Although Leonard often disclaims the role of detective work in his stories, police detective Cal Brown is every bit as good as Edgar Allan Poe's

Dupin when he divulges his 100 percent correct theory to Emory Parks, a clever "little fat black assistant from the prosecutor's office" (166): "Maybe somebody came in the day before . . . and picked up another dolly box with a mark on it, but they don't tell Mr. Stickley. He's supposed to come out, they open the box and they say, Yeah—giving him the dead eyes—now where's the real stuff? But he doesn't come out. He looks around and he's got a forty-four Mag in his ass" (169).

Unable to be held on anything more serious than a shoplifting charge, Stick finds himself soon released on bail, but he is aware that Cal Brown and Emory Parks are on to him, and worse, that Sportree and Leon Woody are ready to kill him lest in order to save his own neck he divulge their complicity in a robbery that caused two deaths.

The pace of the story increases noticeably from this point as chapter sections grow shorter, and Leonard hastens *Swag* to its one-two punch conclusion. First there is a double double cross when Stick shoots the two black gangsters who have lured him and Frank to them meaning to kill them. In the Ritz Motel on Woodward Avenue, Stick shoots both Sportree and Leon Woody with a Luger he has concealed on his person at the moment Leon comes out of a bathroom, "the towel wrapped around his hand, around something in his hand" (*Swag,* 214).

This penultimate scene is followed by a typical ironic ending. Arlene, now Stick's girl and confidante, has been entrusted with the retrieved money and charged to buy them all tickets to Florida because the boys themselves are under close police surveillance. But at the airport, the simple young woman has second thoughts about deeper involvement with Stick versus a career that just might take her to Hollywood. Instead of following the plan, she flies off to Los Angeles for a modeling gig, leaving behind an envelope with the message "I'm sorry" and keys to the locker where she has put the swag. Moments later, the cops, led by Cal Brown, descend on the two and find the envelope. Frank and Stick are done for in a story that Newgate Callendar called succinctly "one of the best of the year."[6]

Booze and Homicide

In *Unknown Man # 89* (1977), Leonard returns to Jack Ryan, last seen in *The Big Bounce*—a very different guy from Al Rosen of *The Hunted,* in Israel and published right after *Swag. Unknown Man* is much more rewarding than *Bounce* or *Hunted,* but it holds up less well than *52 Pick-Up* or *Swag* because of a dated touchy-feely quality. Both Jack Ryan and his girl Denise Leary are wont to wax enthusiastic about the principles of Alcoholics Anonymous, to which Leonard belonged at the time. She tends to assert things like *"No More Bullshit.* . . . I love that. I think I'll paint it on my wall" or "I love whales."[7] Where is Nancy Hayes, Jack Ryan's vicious squeeze from *The Big Bounce,* when we need her?

Some of this sort of thing seems to reflect Leonard's own midlife crisis, though how much remains uncertain. Whether he felt about his own first marriage as Jack Ryan does is moot: "He had gone by the book and purposely picked a sweet June Allyson and discovered too late that when you take the girl next door into a different life she isn't the girl next door anymore. So he said fuck it—going through the motions of playing house, being someone he didn't want to be—and got a divorce" (*Unknown,* 6). At any rate, Leonard, like Ryan, slipped several times from sobriety before going on the wagon permanently, and the language he uses in interviews and conversations echoes Jack's. In a set speech of more than a page, Ryan first tells Denise that he's "been very happy in the last couple of years. Not only because I've been sober and feel better physically, but because the program has changed my attitude" (121). Then he talks about a guy "with an advertising agency" whose self-honesty and sobriety inspire him, a friend who sounds suspiciously like Leonard himself:

> I know I can be myself. I don't have to play a role, put up a front, pretend to be something I'm not. I even listen to what people say now. I can argue without getting mad. If the other person gets mad, that's his problem. I don't feel the need to convince everybody I'm right. Somebody said here tonight, "I like myself now, and it's good to be able to say that." I had fun drinking, I'll admit it. At least I had fun for about ten or twelve years and, fortunately, I didn't get in too much trouble or hit bottom or sleep in the weeds. (121)

The plot of *Unknown Man # 89,* even the title, harkens back to the complicated noir films of the forties that left as much unanswered as accounted for, though the novel is packed with original Leonard touches. Jack Ryan, now 36 years old and a process server in Detroit, is hired to find a mysterious figure. In the tested noir tradition, this search by an "almost" private eye brings Jack to a host of low haunts and in contact with some bizarre folk as he rubs shoulders with cops, thugs, and a "soiled" woman.

Jack is looking for Robert Leary Jr. on behalf of F. X. Perez of New Orleans, he eventually learns. Perez and his Cajun flunkie Raymond

Gidre go straight back to *The Maltese Falcon,* though Gidre's character
has more Richard Widmark and Dual Meaders of *The Moonshine War* in
it than Elisha Cook Jr.

Ryan finds the search more difficult than he had anticipated. But
with the help of a Detroit police contact, he is led to the man's wife.
Robert Leary (aka Bobby Lear) is a psychotic black hoodlum who had
been left Denver Pacific stock years ago by his father, the faithful
retainer of a prosperous white family. But someone else is after Bobby,
Virgil Royal. Fresh out of prison, Virgil is convinced that Bobby has a
pile of money from the Wyandotte Savings stickup the two pulled and
for which Virgil did time. Things grow more convoluted as Ryan begins
to fall for Bobby Lear's abandoned lush of a wife Leann (a white girl now
called Denise), and when Virgil murders Bobby, who becomes briefly
the morgue's unknown man number 89. In the tradition of film noir,
Unknown Man teems with betrayals, and almost everyone might be
characterized as dysfunctional. Ryan and Leann (Denise) manage to
escape the morass through AA and remain faithful to each other,
redeemed not so much by love as by being fundamentally decent,
always Leonard's ultimate ethic. The villainous F. X. Perez, who is certain that the two mean to cheat him out of his fee (either alone or
together), comes through nearly unscathed as well, but his survival is in
accordance with Leonard's second law of thermodynamics—he's beginning to like the guy.

The book concludes with the usual little twist. Much of the story has
involved a suitcase stuffed with Perez's papers stolen from his hotel
room by Virgil and Tunafish, his brother-in-law. In his most noir novels,
Leonard often resorts to the device of something that must be recovered,
a typewriter in *LaBrava* or a gun in *City Primeval,* his version of the Maltese falcon statuette. In this instance, Ryan gets to the suitcase before
Perez and finds out the name of the stock Denise will inherit as the
legitimate heir of the late Bobby Lear. Further, Ryan offers to sell Perez
photocopies of the contents of the suitcase without which Perez cannot
conduct business. If it seems slightly hokey that Perez has no duplicate
records or cannot remember any of his transactions, so be it. Few readers
will object.

Attention to detail is a matter of pride with Leonard, but he always
admits that his plots are less than infallible. Oddly enough, he is much
more defensive about matters of documentation. *Booklist* complimented
him for his depiction of "the ways of process serving" in *Unknown Man*
in a favorable review some years before he employed a research assistant,

and even Marguerite Harper (in her first letter to him) had expressed admiration at the authenticity of his Apache lore. But mistakes do creep in. For example, in *Swag,* he mentions a safety on Stick's Smith and Wesson Chief's Special (which has none), or he confuses the Walther P38 with the Luger, both German military pistols.[8] In *Unknown Man,* a cop's .357 Magnum is "almost as big as Clint Eastwood's." But Dirty Harry packed a .44 Magnum, not a .357. None of these things matters much, however, for God is not in the details in fiction. Rather, it is the appearance of reality that counts, and there Leonard doesn't let us down.

One of the most exciting scenes in *Unknown Man* is Virgil's murder of Bobby Lear at the fleabag Montcalm Hotel.[9] To prepare, Virgil sneaks down the fire escape and leaves his sawed-off 12 gauge shotgun on the windowsill of Bobby's bathroom. Then he knocks on the door and is allowed to enter by Bobby, who frisks him and keeps him covered the whole time with a nickel-plated .38 revolver. When it becomes clear to Virgil there is no chance he will recover from Bobby any money from the Wyandotte Savings holdup, Virgil turns toward the bathroom. "Where are you going?" Bobby asks. "Make wee-wee. That all right?" It better be all right, or the scene is lost. Inside, Virgil retrieves the gun, and comes out shooting (*Unknown,* 96). Leonard had used the bathroom trick before in *Swag* and would again in *Cat Chaser.* But who's counting? Even if he borrowed it from *The Godfather*—as he probably did—it works.

The book's last bloodbath is equally well done. It revolves on the turning over of that suitcase to Raymond Gidre by Virgil and Tunafish in exchange for a large payment. Of course, no one has any intention of keeping his word—the *Hombre* scenario, again. The meeting place for the transaction is the Watts Club in Detroit, where Virgil arrives first to choreograph the showdown. But all is in vain. Raymond ignores any of the diplomatic niceties Virgil expected him to observe and, after ordering a drink, simply shoots Tunafish in the face. Virgil's reaction to all this is our own dazzled confusion: "He . . . couldn't believe what was happening" (*Unknown,* 239).

Kidnapping Gone Wrong

The Switch, Leonard's next novel, is another Detroit kidnapping story, but it is a variation on *52 Pick-Up,* since instead of a husband fighting criminals to get his wife back, Fred Dawson is delighted to let wife Mickey go.[10] In return, Mickey Dawson becomes Leonard's version of Ibsen's

Nora in *A Doll's House*. Much of the novel—perhaps too much—concerns the relationship between an obnoxious and dishonest Bloomfield Hills executive and his long-suffering wife, whose revolt is triggered by something similar to what psychologists call the Stockholm Syndrome, a sympathy she develops for her captors during the days she is held a prisoner by Ordell Robbie and Louis Gara at the house of Richard Edgar Monk at 1035 State Fair, at the edge of Detroit City limits.

Monk is the sort of nonentity we read about in the newspapers, a wannabe cop with a security service. He lives alone in what was his mother's house in a neighborhood where aluminum awnings, statues of the Virgin Mary, and plastic flamingos don't bring condescending grins. But his right-wing views don't hold him back from taking a weekly payoff from Ordell Robbie for closing his eyes to Ordell's burglaries at sites Monk is supposed to be guarding. Monk collects the sort of Nazi memorabilia referred to as "relics" at gun shows: "several grenades, bayonets, trench knives, a gas mask, an Afrika Korps soft hat, Nazi armbands," and photographs of the likes of Hitler and Heinrich Himmler, an impressive hoard financed on a wage of $3.65 an hour, (*Switch,* 40). In addition, Monk possesses a small arsenal of deadly weapons.

Fat and smelly, with a crew cut and vacant blue eyes, the son of a mother who had him saying rosaries for the conversion of Russia, Richard Edgar Monk provides a splendid vignette of the balmy confusions of late-twentieth-century America and testimony to Leonard's uncanny ability to find the country's pulse—or at least that of its substantial lunatic fringe—in a page or two of carefully crafted prose.

One might imagine that a black man like Ordell Robbie would harbor some uncharitable feelings toward a reader of *Thunderbolt,* with its hostile racist articles. Richard Monk's view toward blacks at its kindest calls for their deportation to Africa. But Ordell Robbie's attitude toward Richard is amazingly tolerant, though still characterized mainly by amused contempt and disbelief. Ordell takes the same kind of pleasure in introducing Richard to Louis Gara when the twosome is considering a location to stash potential kidnap victim Mickey Dawson as an entomologist takes in showing off a loathsome insect.

Ordell is a perceptive social critic as well. On the guided tour of Detroit he gives Louis, he remarks that Coleman Young, Detroit's black mayor, "got to fix this city up." He contrasts the expensive cosmetic measures taken along the river, "the glass shit and convention center and domes" that he dismisses as stuff for "postcard pictures," with stretches of Woodward Avenue: "What does anybody want to come here for? Pick up some ribs and leave the motor running" (*Switch*, 17). Later, in the area near the Wayne State campus, they drive by a community demonstration against street prostitution where pickets hold up signs reading, "HONK YOUR HORN IF YOU SUPPORT US." "Trying to keep the neighborhood from falling in the trash can," he explains to Louis, and Leonard adds, "Ordell beeped a couple of times and waved" (19).

The plan is to kidnap Mickey and demand ransom money from her husband, who buys stolen merchandise from Ordell (though he scarcely recognizes him) to outfit buildings he buys on margin and rents to pimps and prostitutes for cash. This money goes unreported to the IRS into a numbered account in the Bahamas, where Ordell has contacts who have discovered the scheme.

What Ordell doesn't know is that the Dawson marriage is on the verge of collapse, and that Frank is planning, on the very weekend of the scheduled kidnapping, to have his wife served with divorce papers so that he can marry a blouse-bursting 21 year old named Melanie whom he visits regularly in the Caribbean.

Just as in *52 Pick-Up*, a predatory male lurks about, hoping to take advantage of the marital discord. Marshall Taylor inadvertently stumbles in on the kidnapping and is pistol-whipped and locked in a closet, but when he gets free, he does nothing about contacting the police for fear he will compromise himself. In the meantime, the kidnappers call Frank, in Freeport with Melanie, demanding that he transfer a million dollars from his secret account to theirs. Like Marshall Taylor, he does nothing, either.

Because the caper is a failure, there is little to say about it, and Leonard must look to his characters. Frank is depicted as a narcissistic male chauvinist, easy to hate but lacking complexity. His son Bo, much like him, is a self-centered teenage tennis hopeful. One of Leonard's few juveniles, Bo is dispatched to his grandparents' home in Fort Lauderdale in an early chapter and not seen again. Thus apart from the heavies, it is Mickey who carries much of the weight of the narrative.

Mickey's initial role is the woman in distress. She is threatened by the creepy Richard, who bores peepholes in the bathroom door and in the door of the bedroom in his house where she is kept. His attempt to rape her goes awry, and his subsequent reaction—firing his treasured Colt Python .357 Magnum at a fleeing Mickey and her rescuer, Louis— brings a police response ending in Richard's death.

When Ordell takes himself off to the Bahamas to deal with Frank, the care and guarding of Mickey is left to Louis. Although no actual romance develops between them, a ticklish situation does. Leonard is obliged to portray sympathetically a randy male ex-con with nearly total power over a more than usually appealing captive. Despite a false alarm or two, he succeeds, and a bond develops between the pair. In *Out of Sight,* Leonard would approach the topic again but suggest that the genuine attraction felt between U.S. Marshal Karen Sisco and the 47-year-old escaped convict Jack Foley must be of brief duration.

The Switch, dedicated to Leonard's mother and to "another Mickey," his new wife Joan Shepard, repeats the women's liberation theme of *52 Pick-Up* in demonstrating how another subservient wife can empower herself. Mickey's liberation comes about via a good deal of seventies style consciousness-raising, and her success is evidenced dubiously by puffing away furiously at marijuana cigarettes, not counting her drinks, and hanging about with a criminal element, the very activities Denise Leary of *Unknown Man* abandoned in her quest for freedom. At one point in her conversion, Mickey even recounts to a dazed Louis her single proletarian experience, five weeks as a salesgirl at Saks Fifth Avenue, a tale that would be preposterous if Mickey herself lacked the acumen to recognize it as such. In addition, Leonard faces the problem of presenting Ordell and Louis favorably, especially after Ordell's shameless betrayal of his partner.

When he realizes he will be unable to collect a million-dollar ransom for a wife Frank Dawson would gladly be rid of, Ordell secretly telephones Richard Monk and tells him to kill "the Jew lady." (Mickey is a Catholic, but Ordell feels Richard needs added incentive.) The new idea—Melanie's, actually—is to provide a slighter service to Frank for the reduced rate of $100,000.

Later, the irrepressible Ordell is appropriately apologetic for the lapse, and all is forgiven. The novel concludes mischievously with a new idea: the boys abetted by Mickey will kidnap Melanie—now practically an auxiliary gang member—and see if Frank will shell out for her return.

Servant of God

Touch, written in 1978 (though not published until 1987, when *Glitz* made Leonard's material suddenly more valuable), draws on his AA experience, as did *Unknown Man # 89* of the previous year. Neither crime fiction nor Western, *Touch* has not had much appeal to the majority of Leonard's readers, who do not find in the book what they look to him for. Nonetheless this story of a stigmatic in the American Catholic Church of the post–Vatican II era actually melds a number of elements perennially attractive to Leonard himself.

Although we usually think of him as a strictly realistic writer because of his painstaking documentation, gritty dialogue, and fiercely contemporary settings, many of Leonard's novels draw on fantastic elements and reveal an interest in modes that distort reality. *Forty Lashes,* for example, roamed a long way from the traditional Western with its imaginative depiction of a will to power, spurred on by an eccentric man of faith, the prison warden at Yuma. *Gunsights* and *Bounty Hunters* both draw on a fantasy element of the folk rising up against monied interests and achieving victory, their energies channeled by an inexplicable force. In *Gold Coast,* Karen DiCilia identifies with Virginia Hill, Bugsy Siegel's moll, and maintains a shrine to her just as Harry Arno in *Pronto* identifies with the poet Ezra Pound and reveres relics of the man. Such veneration is a powerful force, closely related to ineffable religious experiences and appealing to both the sophisticated and the simple.

Leonard has never rejected the miraculous or the religion in which he was raised, with its central doctrine of the Incarnation, of God becoming a human being, which Leonard is capable of seeing as metaphorically as Emerson. His experiences in AA intensified his conviction that a spiritual force infuses lives as he successfully put drinking behind him, assisted by an openly acknowledged religious organization.

Further, he grew up attending parochial schools in an era and a city where ultraconservative views of a quasi-religious nature received wide attention, whether in Henry Ford's anti-Semitic *Dearborn Independent* or on the air by the Reverend Charles Edward Coughlin, broadcasting from the Shrine of the Little Flower, whose long shadow extended into every corner of Catholic life in Detroit until silenced by the church in 1942. Leonard remembers his schoolmates hawking Coughlin's *Social Justice* on Sundays after mass in front of Blessed Sacrament. Although his own weltanschauung is far from that of Coughlin or Pound—who also took to the airwaves on behalf of fascism—Leonard retains a fascination with those whose twisted convictions served the menacing figures abroad in the world at that time.

In *Touch,* Juvenal (whose real name is Charlie Lawson) has left the Franciscan Order with which he was a brother stationed in South America to work with alcoholics at a center in Detroit. Here he is discovered by Bill Hill, a genial but none too honest former evangelist selling RVs. He and others try to capitalize on Juvenal's power to heal. Although

Touch is not a crime story, August Murray, a deranged reactionary Catholic activist and leader of the Gray Army of the Holy Ghost, packs a .38 and is ready to kill. Determined to reverse the direction of the Catholic Church in recent years, Murray needs Juvenal in his movement and is determined to break up the young man's budding relationship with Lynn Faulkner.

Despite the up-to-date Detroit setting, the characterization of Juvenal draws on the tradition of the "holy fool," a Christlike figure who has attracted other writers, notably Gerhart Hauptmann in *The Fool in Christ* (1911). Of childlike faith, this mystic's belief and love transcend all schemes and human ambitions. As such, he—or often she—lives the *imitatio Christi* achieved by saints such as Francis of Assisi, for example; others like Catherine of Siena or the Little Flower (Theresa of Avila), while also indifferent to secular and ecclesiastic ambitions, showed no hesitation about criticizing the church or challenging its hierarchy.

We seldom encounter Juvenal's point of view, but rather the reaction to him of those around him, mainly Lynn, not because Leonard loses interest in him (as he would with Karen DiCilia in *Gold Coast* or had with Al Rosen in *The Hunted*) but because Juvenal's essence must remain a mystery. Juvenal's relationship with Lynn is depicted as sexual, since Leonard wants him to be seen as a fully rounded human being, not a bloodless ascetic; but the effect is not entirely successful, as though the pope were to announce a serious interest in Meryl Streep.

Even the book's villain, August Murray, a Detroit printer with the soul of the Grand Inquisitor, fails to stir the blood; and his punishment is only to be healed on Howard Hart's *Hartline* by Juvenal, who had earlier pushed Murray off a balcony when he attempted to shoot Lynn. August Murray's desire to return to a pre–Vatican II world of Latin liturgy and theological certainties doesn't seem terribly hateful. His energies are merely misdirected. The fellow craves respect and longs for order. When Juvenal restores him to health before a national TV audience, the reader wonders if August (now shorn of his pride) couldn't profitably be employed in some new and harmless venture. His organizational skills, endless drive, and total lack of humor must qualify him for numerous positions in the American workplace.

Leonard's tolerance of, and impatience with, zealotry are put to good use in *Touch*. He provides a colorful picture of Catholic confusion in the seventies in counterpoint to a saint's life, revealing that the more things change, the more they remain the same. At the end, when Juvenal goes off on a tryst with Lynn, he is only doing what certain rationalists of the

nineteenth century thought that Jesus was doing with the woman at the
fountain. At any rate, the couple is headed for Luckenbach, Texas, where
Waylon Jennings convinced the decade that traditional values flourish
unimpaired.

High Noon Meets The Big Sleep

Leonard often refers to *City Primeval* (1980), bearing the subtitle *High
Noon in Detroit,* as an "urban Western." Written directly after *Gunsights,*
it borrows a number of effects from the Westerns, so that the result is
often like *High Noon* meets *The Big Sleep.* Detroit appears again as the
meeting place of elemental and vicious criminals in loose contact with
the monied class that profits from their existence while the cops range in
between. But this idea does not find as distinct an expression as in
52 Pick-Up or *The Switch* because Leonard is more attracted by a depiction of good guys versus bad guys in Western fashion, and in trying to
demonstrate in a slightly contradictory manner that police and crooks
have more in common than not. Of course, the notion that police and
criminals share common ground goes back at least to Victor Hugo's *Les
Misérables* (1862). But in *City Primeval* this idea is articulated by the psychotic Clement Mansell. It never finds really coherent expression, since
the cops are all pretty decent guys, nothing like Clement.

Instead of locating one group inside the city limits and the other in
upscale neighborhoods outside, Leonard brings them together, frequently in the high-rise apartments of the never seen Del Weems, the
guy currently keeping Sandy Stanton. From there, the landmarks of
Detroit, among them the always ironically used Renaissance Center, can
be seen, as well as distant Windsor just across the Detroit River in
Ontario. Leonard uses the same vistas in *Out of Sight,* which Steven
Soderbergh kept in the film version to great effect. There, the city is
shown glittering below in one of Leonard's most effective love scenes,
and later wrapped in a blanket of falling snow that cannot conceal its
festering corruption.

While leaning heavily on the cop experience acquired during his
weeks at 1300 Beaubien, and showing a familiarity with police routine
and jargon greater than in any book hitherto, Leonard still manages to
work in plenty of Western allusions. Even the characters seem aware of
the sustaining structure of the story and sprinkle their talk with words
like "duel" and "mano a mano," as well as making references to numerous oaters.[11]

The duel will be between the "Oklahoma Wildman" Clement Mansell (transplanted to Detroit) and Acting Detective Sergeant Raymond Cruz, of Mexican descent (who came, like Leonard, as a child of 10 to Detroit). Raymond is another recently divorced protagonist, watching his pennies and trying to find some direction to his life. Clement formerly belonged to a gang called the Wrecking Crew, which broke into crack houses and robbed them. When the gang went to jail, Clement's lawyer, Carolyn Wilder, got him released on a technicality. She is the typical Leonard woman of later books: sexy, career oriented, self-reliant, and smart as a whip. Leonard creates a complex character who is invariably a liberal, even annoyingly politically correct, but is also the product of parochial schools and Catholic colleges and is devoted to her father.

Like Hemingway or Fitzgerald before him, Leonard is both turned on by, and wary of, the "new woman." The reader, on the other hand, may be wondering why a hotshot like Carolyn Wilder, who lives in an elegantly remodeled town house, represents a psychotic indigent (she does not seem to be court appointed or concerned with pro bono work, and she continues as Clement's lawyer even after his original indictment is dismissed). Her scheme of allowing her client to serve time on a minor federal conviction, assuming that the City of Detroit will fail to bring him to trial within 180 days, works; but her reward is to suffer a beating at Clement's hands. At that point, she washes her hands of him. It's hard not to imagine that this Wonder Woman is not being meted out a bit of auctorial punishment for overreaching, since the real reason she stays with Clement is her overweening pride. She is convinced she can handle him.

City Primeval opens in the compelling movie style that Leonard brings to many of his books, especially the later ones, when he has film possibilities firmly in mind. Clement has been planning to rob an Albanian American whom his girlfriend Sandy Stanton has been cultivating for this purpose. Clement's idea is to follow the couple back from the Hazel Park Racecourse to the guy's place in Hamtramck and stick a gun in his face, but he is distracted by a black man driving a Lincoln Mark VI with a white woman in the front seat. This is Judge Alvin Guy, a flashy egomaniac whose outrageous courtroom shenanigans have won him the enmity of half the city's blacks and all its whites. A prologue to the book provides a rundown of the judge's career. A sort of capsule history of any number of recent jurists we have read about who flourish mostly in decayed cities like Coleman Young's Detroit, the prologue provides a gripping contemporary portrait of a dangerous man able to manipulate racial discord to his own advantage.

Equally gripping and faithful is the depiction of what we now glibly call "road rage," as Clement sideswipes the judge's car and chases it through deserted streets, bumping it from behind until the older man seeks refuge in an empty parking lot, where Clement calmly shoots him through the windshield multiple times with his Walther P38, having still no idea who the man is. When his plan to make the woman passenger take him to the judge's house for more thorough pilfering goes awry, he shoots her, too.

Police are called in to solve the double murder, and Raymond Cruz's suspicions focus immediately on Clement, whose history is familiar to Raymond, and whose presence at the racetrack can be partially corroborated by witnesses. Ballistic evidence soon establishes that the murder weapon was a 9 mm Walther P38, a gun that Clement is known to have had in his possession.[12] This pistol plays a large role in the story as Raymond attempts to tie him to it and Clement tries to get rid of it.

The device of a cop locked in a personal vendetta with a criminal is a favorite of TV shows and movies. Although this is awfully rare in real life, films like *Cape Fear* (1962) and *Tightrope* (1984) have capitalized on the innate suspense generated by the situation and the conventions it entails: the lawman playing by the rules, and the criminal (usually a particularly vicious and deranged one) ignoring them. Often the criminal menaces a loved one of the cop (here Carolyn Wilder would qualify) or threatens the policeman's off-duty life by invading his home (as when Clement fires a .22 Ruger rifle at Raymond through his apartment window).

The scene is chilling and vaguely sexual with its voyeuristic overtones and suggestion of a piercing by the phallic gun. But then Leonard reminds the reader that the phallus is "a regular $87.50 value for $69.95 . . . at K-Mart," the sort of wild deadpan comment that endears him and lifts him above the competition (*City*, 103). Detroit is just another name for Gomorrha.

Although the drama of the obsessed cop relentlessly pursuing the criminal works well in *City Primeval,* the ancillary notion that the legality of the pursuit is of minor importance is far less credible. Clement says to Raymond at one point: "You don't set out to uphold the law any more'n I set out to break it" (*City*, 88). That statement has a nice "Western" flavor to it, as if two natural men, one decent and one evil, were just fulfilling their instincts. But Raymond always behaves ethically. He may bend the law a bit, as he does to trap Clement at the end, but he does not thumb his nose at it. John Russell of *Hombre,* who gave his life for others, saw no reason to handicap himself in his struggle with the innate evil of Frank Braden. Russell's question to Braden, "How are you going to get down that hill?" (*Hombre,* 157), resonates in *City Primeval,* too. Clement is simply wrong when he says to Raymond: "Me and you start playing a game. You try and catch me and I try and keep from getting caught" (*City,* 88). It's not a game. If you behave like the devil, you become him. The end does not justify the means. Leonard learned that lesson from the Jesuits and the example of Hitler, whose baleful presence in the world left an impact of immeasurable depth on the young serviceman, and on everyone else who came of age in his time. The truly evil never walk away unscathed in Leonard's books, though the mean and nasty do time and time again.

To catch Clement, who openly defies him, Raymond needs the assistance of his girlfriend, Sandy Stanton, and his attorney, Carolyn Wilder. At first, both women rebuff him, but Carolyn's frosty advocacy melts when her client attempts to blackmail and brutalize her; and Sandy yields to Raymond's offer of protection from a man she fears. Her capitulation is not vastly different from Carolyn's in that both prove vulnerable to Raymond's charm, strength, and sensitivity. A sister under the skin, Sandy is another of those airheads whom Leonard draws with unfailing accuracy. A cocktail waitress who wanders aimlessly from man to man, she is now in an abusive relationship with Clement, who has instructed her to dump his Walther P38 into the Detroit River. Instead, she trades the gun to Mr. Sweety, a black bar owner, for the marijuana she depends on to soothe her nerves. Mr. Sweety, with great good sense, betrays her to the cops to save his own neck. When Raymond comes to question her, she is smoking dope and watching *The Newlyweds Game.* In the ensuing scene, Leonard conveys her vulnerability and satirizes American life. Trying desperately to focus her clouded mind on Raymond's questions while distracted by a TV show to which she looks for moral guidance, Sandy answers aloud the emcee's question about whom she'd like to "make whoopee" with and whom she'd like to marry: "Gregory Peck." (Robert Redford is her "whoopee" choice.) "A young Gregory Peck," she adds. "He's so calm. You want to know something? When you first came here, the first time, you reminded me of him. A younger Gregory Peck—that's what I thought of" (*City,* 173).

Before Raymond can get the elusive P38 back into Clement's hands, Leonard provides several episodes with "the Albanians," an exotic component of Detroit's ethnic mix. They, too, are after Clement for his mutilation and robbery of one of their number, the 34-year-old Skender Lulgjaraj, whom Sandy has been setting up at Clement's urging. Here James Russell Lowell's remarks about Fenimore Cooper seem apropos:

> His Indians with proper respect be it said
> Are just Natty Bumppo daubed over with red.[13]

The Albanians who try unsuccessfully to bushwhack Clement in front of Carolyn Wilder's house speak a stilted English, endorse a primitive code of honor, and practice a clannishness marked by blood feud (always called "the custom"). Led by Toma, their chief, they are, of course, urban Apaches roaming the streets and lending another bit of Western flavor to *High Noon in Detroit.*

The Albanian plot provides Leonard the opportunity to introduce a secret room hidden by a revolving door, no doubt the legacy of boyhood reading. That Carolyn Wilder's housekeeper is a murderess, a former client who once killed her husband, suggests that Leonard also remembers Mr. Jaggers's murderous housekeeper in *Great Expectations.* Everything is grist for the mill for this omnivorous reader.

True to his word, Don Fine at Arbor House got this taut new story to big-time reviewers, and sales shot up. But *City Primeval* had no need of hype to promote its genuine merits, and the public began to discover what a treasure had been around for a long time. Leonard's craftsmanship in *City Primeval* greatly surpasses that of *The Switch* or *52 Pick-Up.* Most readers, unaware of the Western touches that Leonard regarded as meaningful, saw only an authoritative big-city crime story with a satirical edge, Panasonic dialogue, a rich cast, and a delicately adumbrated romance.

The Favorite

After *City Primeval* Leonard left Detroit settings for close to a decade, not returning until *Freaky Deaky* (1988). Although Raymond Cruz and policewoman Maureen Downey make cameo appearances, *Freaky Deaky* is not really a cop novel, even though Chris Mankowski, a Polish American Detroiter, is a police detective. Similar to other Leonard protagonists, though tougher, he is frequently perceived by others as an "old-time dick," the sort of cop who once used a blackjack and cut corners. But Mankowski is deceptive in this respect. Although not above taking a shortcut, he behaves as honestly as Raymond Cruz or Vincent Mora. Before allowing Skip Gibb and Robin Abbott, the superannuated hippie heavies of *Freaky Deaky,* to be blown to smithereens, Mankowski offers them the opportunity to surrender. Since they have no inkling of what is about to occur and are holding all the cards at the moment, they naturally ignore him. Mankowski knows they will but warns the pair, "I have to give you a chance. You don't take it, it's up to you."[14] His reputation is a vestige of a less enlightened era and allows Robin, Skip, and Donnell Lewis to believe he is on the take. Their error, their conviction that he is ready to be bribed, gives him an inside line to their criminal schemes.

Measured by any standard, *Freaky Deaky* is a dazzler. The plot may wander a bit, but Leonard convinces us that this is the fault of Robin and her accomplice Skip, who keep changing their minds about their goals. Robin and Skip run into each other years after both flourished as student radicals of the seventies. They have both done time for blowing up an army recruiting office in the Detroit Federal Building on 29 September 1971. Now Skip works for the movies, often as a demolition expert. Robin, "almost forty," the meaner and more dangerous of these two loose cannons, has written four "historical romance-rape" novels (*Freaky,* 18). Their caper, modified several times, is to shake down wealthy Mark Ricks (or his even wealthier, fat, alcoholic brother) for $700,000, suspecting the brothers fingered them to the FBI years ago. The background of these characters provides Mankowski an opportunity to supply us a pocket history of the Vietnam War years in America:

> I try to remember the way it was . . . and I get it mixed up with the way it was shown in movies, with the hippies so much wiser and laid back than the straights. Except in the Woodstock movie where the young guy says, "People who are nowhere come here because they think they're gonna be with people who are somewhere." And the guy's dopey girlfriend doesn't get it. She says, "Yeah, well, like there's plenty of freedom. We ball and everything. . . ." She was being used and didn't know it. You saw so much of that. All kinds of dumb kids taken advantage of by guys pretending to be gurus or Jesus, they had the hair, the beard. Or some asshole who called himself the Pussycat Prince and wore flowers in his hair and played a flute. All of them with that smug, stoned grin, like they knew something you didn't. (*Freaky,* 232)

The book starts with one of those bangers Leonard often uses—in this case literally, since a thug named Booker is blown to pieces when he gets up from a chair, activating an explosive device. This incident has little to do with the main story, however, except to introduce dynamite as a weapon, Chris Mankowski of the bomb squad, and a black hood named Juicy Mouth (who will undoubtedly appear in another Leonard novel someday). The real stars of *Freaky Deaky* are Donnell Lewis and Woody Ricks. Not since Vivien Leigh played Scarlett O'Hara and Hattie McDaniel her mammy has there been a more diverting master-servant relationship. But Donnell is no Hattie, though he flatters "the man" constantly and caters to his bizarre demands. Totally in control of his self-indulgent, narcissistic boss, Donnell is grooming the infantile Woody for the fleecing of his life. A crook from the word go, Donnell is still widely appealing, and as the book progresses, Leonard grows to love him as much as Dreiser loved Sister Carrie. In typical fashion, Leonard began by picturing a bad guy but changed his mind as early as chapter 9, when Mankowski has his first run-in with Donnell and has to admit that he's a "stand-up guy" (*Freaky,* 88).[15]

As Mr. Woody's indispensable factotum, Donnell manages to get rid of the other servants. (Leonard, who often has a movie or two running around in his head—*Lethal Weapon* receives mention in *Freaky Deaky*—may have had memories of Dirk Bogarde in *The Servant*.) Woody was his late mother's favorite, and after the death of his brother, blown up by a bomb meant for Woody himself, he inherits the fortune of his entrepreneur dad, a deceased tycoon. Although he rapes Greta Wyatt, Mankowski's love interest, Woody is depicted as harmless for the most part and spends his days eating peanuts, drinking large quantities of alcohol, listening to show tunes, and floating naked in his huge indoor pool. Donnell, we learn, "had been doing most of the man's thinking for the past three years" (*Freaky,* 134), a job that keeps him occupied, since "if the man was any dumber you'd have to water him twice a week" (213).

A former Black Panther, Donnell is now more a nursemaid. But even if he plans to rip off his charge at the first opportunity, he manages to show something close to affection for the dysfunctional infant rapidly eating and drinking his way to death. Donnell migh be "a well-behaved house nigger" these days, but the reward for his ingenuity and wit is great lines like those spoken when Woody whines that he woke up at night and couldn't find him: "I told you I had to go out, Mr. Woody. My mother had a dream I died and I had to show her I was fine. Then I had to look in the Dream Book for her, see what number it meant to play" (293).

Donnell is seduced by Robin's even more ambitious scheme than his own to get Woody's money, but he is gradually made uneasy by her talent for betrayal. In a story where treachery is almost an art form, Donnell finally throws his lot in with Mankowski as the suspenseful conclusion inside the dreary Gothic mansion approaches. The House of Ricks is split asunder, more or less, when Skip and Robin fall victim to five sticks of Austin Powder before they can get to the bank to cash Woody's check for $1.7 million, a sum supposedly reflecting the sale of rights to Robin's novels.

In *Freaky Deaky* Leonard gives new life to that old TV chestnut about the cop who is suspended from the force but goes on working on the case so that he can vindicate himself. In this story, Mankowski is assisted by a crusty older black cop willing to close his eyes to certain irregularities.

But the book is packed with all the extras that identify Leonard's novels, too. Its satiric bite never falters, whether he is exposing the inequities of American public health in city hospitals (as when Greta calls Detroit General "the scariest hospital I've ever been in . . . people . . . handcuffed to their beds. I think half the patients have gunshot wounds," and Mankowski adds thoughtfully, "Well, some of them" [*Freaky,* 107]), or the injustices of a judicial system that turns its back on sexual assault if the perpetrator is a wealthy white man. Mankowski's interview with a police psychiatrist (whose degrees are all from Wayne State) turns into an attack on Freudian fundamentalism and know-it-all authorities. The shrink reaches the conclusion that the detective is bisexual because he doesn't like spiders, the same charge a smarmy female reporter makes about Raymond Cruz in *City Primeval*.

The title *Freaky Deaky* comes from an uninhibited ghetto dance, fun to do but sexy and dangerous: "You freaky deaky with someone else's woman you could get seriously hurt" (*Freaky,* 254). At any moment in this book, you can be raped, blown up, or maimed. Courage helps. Mankowski marches into the lion's den without his 17-shot Glock 9 mm a dozen times. He's a stand-up guy with a head on his shoulders. He's fair to Greta and has a good relationship with his dad, the familial test being a Leonard standby. Things have pretty much broken down between him and his ex-girlfriend Phyllis, though. Once he phones her to ask how quickly checks for a large sum of money can be cashed, and she attempts to manipulate his feelings by telling him about "Bob" whom she's just met. Mankowski listens dutifully before delivering the zinger: "Is this Bob by any chance married?" (*Freaky,* 274).

Although he gets depressed like anyone else, Mankowski is remarkably cheerful most of the time; no cosmic ennui threatens him when he prowls dangerous streets, like the old-time dicks he resembles, going from sleazy bars to parking lots where hoods wait to break his legs. But his mind rivals those noir gumshoes of the thirties and forties when it comes to detective work. He can figure things out faster than Sam Spade: "Maybe she's mad at somebody," a colleague says to him. "Maybe somebody, when she was busted. . . ." "Yeah, I like it. I might be able to look into that" (*Freaky*, 203).

We might wonder how anyone can cash million-dollar checks, or how Donnell keeps spotting bombs before they go off, or even why Skip's .38 doesn't fall out of his waistband when Mankowski knocks him on his head. But *Freaky Deaky* is all the things reviewers said: "a riveting page-turner," "pungent and funny," a good read, Leonard at his best and his own favorite book. It's tough and realistic, rich in detail, with an array of funky characters. Robin and Skip, those thoroughly rotten love children out to exploit whomever they can, join rascally preachers as genuine American folk figures. When finally these extortionists are hoist by their own petard in Woody's creepy library, every reader will sigh in relief.

Home Alone

Killshot (1989) reached the best-seller list boosted by the phenomenal success of *Glitz* and to a lesser extent *Freaky Deaky*, though not much by *Bandits,* a weaker effort. Nonetheless the influence of *Bandits* is strongly present in Leonard's creation of Armand Degas, the Blackbird, a half Objibway whose mind is full of the same primitive mystic currents that concerned Franklin de Dios in the earlier novel (or Nestor Soto of *Stick,* for that matter).

Killshot is a frightening book about two "fucking maniacs." The first is the Bird, named for a childhood incident at the Indian reservation on Walpole Island, across Lake St. Clair from Detroit, when Armand's grandmother told him she could turn him into a bird. The second is the garrulous Richie Nix, another grinning, impetuous, unreliable Richard Widmark type.

Unlike most of Leonard's crime stories, *Killshot* provides little traditional plot. In fact, a defect of the novel is the lack of motivation for the events of the story. In *Freaky Deaky,* when the plot wavered, it could be attributed to Robin Abbott's changing her mind, but in *Killshot* even Richie Nix must acknowledge that there is no reason for what he and the Bird are doing: "There wasn't a dime to be made off it."[16]

What they are doing is trying to kill Wayne and Carmen Colson, a couple in their late thirties, who live in a rural area outside of Detroit. Wayne is an ironworker, and Carmen (named after Guy Lombardo's brother, by the way) has just begun to sell real estate.

The Bird is a for-hire killer sometimes employed by the Toronto Mafia, though why that organization should turn to a half-French, half-Indian psychopath is puzzling enough for a character in the story to ask that question, too. The Bird meets Richie Nix outside a restaurant where Richie is planning to steal his car. In a scene close to one used in *Swag,* Richie soon finds himself telling the Bird, "You're just the guy I'm looking for" (*Killshot,* 50). Their first operation together will be to carry out a harebrained extortion scheme Richie has thought up to shake down a local real estate man. Fresh out of prison with a long rap sheet including several murders behind him, Richie is living with Donna Mulry, years older than he, an Elvis devotee and former state prison cook.

The attempt of the two to collect $10,000 from Nelson Davies brings them into accidental contact with Wayne Colson, who chases them off. From this point on, Richie and the Bird are after the Colsons. When the police prove inept at capturing the duo, who go on a violent crime wave, the Colsons are persuaded to enter the Witness Protection Program and to leave Michigan for Cape Giradeau, Missouri. In taking the story this far, Leonard provides a good deal of information on a variety of topics, ranging from the ironworker's trade to duck hunting, the tricks of the real estate game, and finally some of the ins and outs of the barge and tugboat business on the Mississippi. For the latter, he used the services of Gregg Sutter—after whose house Leonard modeled the Colsons'—dispatched to Cape Giradeau, where Sutter spent days poking about and taking pictures. But Leonard also drew on a nearly forgotten novel he admires by Richard Bissell called *A Stretch on the River.* If remembered at all, Bissell is probably recalled as the author of $7^{1}/_{2}$ *Cents,* on which the popular fifties musical *The Pajama Game* was based. Bissell's wry sense of humor, tolerant attitudes toward human frailties, boundless curiosity, prewar coolness, earthy interest in sex, and joie de vivre have all left their mark on Leonard's work.

Killshot offers a detailed picture of a blue collar marriage, one that recalls Bobbie Ann Mason's vivid short story "Shiloh," which Leonard had read. Wayne is another self-reliant, tough protagonist. Possessed of a short fuse, he is usually considerate of his wife, a woman more than able to hold her own with a guy who hunts and fishes and has a pickup truck and a boat. As usual, Leonard insists that male-female relations flourish best under conditions of equality and good sex. But equality comes first. Neither partner is treated patronizingly by him, though each is vulnerable, Carmen with her trust in handwriting analysis and Wayne with a Tim-the-Toolman mentality.

Their lives, however, are not as compelling as those of the "fucking maniacs," who live for a while in a ménage à trois with Donna Mulry, a creature like those with lacquered hair and rhinestone eyeglasses who sat in Liberace's audiences. A marvel of bad taste, from her stuffed animals to her Elvis memorabilia and her choice of men, she is an instantly recognizable type of American woman.

Again, the book owes to countless movies, some mentioned by name, like Jack Nicholson's *The Passenger* as Carmen tussles with her new identity; some alluded to obliquely, like Charles Bronson's *Death Wish* (1974). But in the final analysis, the novel's greatest debt is to the horror film, the I-am-watching-you—or, scarier yet, the I-am-already-inside-your-house—sort. Leonard uses the house-under-siege theme again but takes it one step farther until it becomes the archetypal fairy tale that frightened us as children. Don't open the door. What can you do if you're home alone and the bad guys get inside?

Such is roughly the pattern of the final scenes of *Killshot*. Carmen has managed to escape a good-old-boy federal marshal in Cape Giradeau who keeps walking in on her with sex on his mind. Now she faces two madmen in her house without her husband. Richie and the Bird resolve to hold her until Wayne returns, though why they don't kill her immediately is not clear. Further, Richie's ideas about sexually assaulting the helpless woman do not proceed very far either—apparently, as in the previous case, from exigencies of plot. At any rate, during the hours of waiting, the Bird kills Richie, reducing the number of Carmen's opponents by half and allowing her to cope with one less nutcase. That she does is a foregone conclusion, but the suspense is maintained till a neat end that doesn't strain our credibility.

Chapter Four
Florida: The Last Resort

Between books set in Michigan, Leonard wrote a new one with a full Florida setting. As early as *The Big Bounce,* he had introduced the teenage terror Nancy Hayes, originally from Florida; and in *Unknown Man # 89,* Jack Ryan and Denise Leary seek brief respite from sanguinary Detroit in the Sunshine State. Now *Gold Coast* (1980), written just before *City Primeval* (though published slightly later), became the first novel with an exclusively Florida background. After *Gold Coast,* Leonard would use Florida settings regularly, though he continued to shift scenes back to Detroit when it suited him.

Since the early forties, Leonard had visited south Florida where he now has a condominium in North Palm Beach. The choice of Florida as the scene for so many of his stories seems more a matter of convenience than a stroke of genius, though it has proved that, too.

Florida's sun-splashed canvas, more fluid society, and Caribbean ambience—not to mention its drug culture—offered Leonard new inspiration. But apart from the novelty and the convenience of writing about an area with which he enjoyed a familiarity equal to that of Detroit, there seems no special significance to his choice of locale. Nevertheless, an increase of regional crime fiction suggests that decadence at least proves inspirational for writers. In recent years, local color has become almost a feature of national crime fiction, and Florida has enjoyed a particularly prominent place in the stories of James W. Hall, Laurence Shames, Edna Buchanan, Carl Hiassen, and John Lutz, impelling students of the genre to ask themselves if Miami has replaced Los Angeles as the capital of homicide. Interestingly enough, actual FBI statistics rate Florida and Michigan as dead equals in the killing business, each boasting a respectable 7.5 murders per 100,000 of population per year.[1]

The Mafia Widow

As he would later in *Killshot,* Leonard draws a bit on fairy-tale motifs in *Gold Coast*. Karen DiCilia, for example, lives alone like a princess, sur-

rounded by wealth, in a huge, castlelike home where she has been shut
up by a wicked, controlling husband and is now threatened by an evil
knight, Roland Crowe, a good old boy out of the swamp who constantly
seeks to invade her home and herself. To "rescue" her, a term she ironically uses several times, appears Cal Maguire, formerly of Detroit.

In the end, she rescues herself by pumping at least four slugs from
her Beretta 9 mm into the overconfident ex-con while Maguire stands
by, jaw agape. Then Karen coolly gives Maguire, who has been doing his
darnedest to assist her, his walking papers: " 'I enjoyed meeting you,'
Karen said. 'Now beat it.' "[2] Karen's brusque farewell will dismay most
readers. Leonard himself sees the problem as arising from his losing
interest again in a character. The story had started with Karen being
depicted as a gutsy lady making the best of a marriage to a sexagenarian
Sicilian American organized crime figure with medieval ideas of the
place of women. But somewhere along the line, Leonard began to think
he would bring Karen in at the last moment during the final confrontation between Roland Crowe and Cal Maguire when an unarmed Cal is
facing a shotgun-wielding Roland at night in the big empty house. As a
result, Karen appears, calmly draws a cigarette out of a pack in her
purse, sits on the corner of a desk, and moments later, as Roland bab-
bles, draws a gun and lets him have it. Real Lauren Bacall stuff. To prepare for this noir conclusion, Leonard was obliged to make his femme
fatale colder and much less sympathetic as the novel progressed.

But the total performance is of such virtuosity that the reader can
overlook a bit of chicanery at the end. Besides, once it was revealed that
Karen possessed a mystery room in the mansion where she kept photographs of herself, the former Karen Hill of Detroit, together with pictures of her look-alike idol, Virginia Hill of gangland fame, we knew
something had to be wrong.[3]

Thirty-six-year-old Calvin Maguire is another marginal guy with a
record of arrests behind him but no convictions. He will remind many of
Jack Ryan in *The Big Bounce,* but we never see Cal actually do anything
nasty, except, of course, stick up the Deep Run Country Club north of
Detroit. This job is performed by Cal and a couple of black brothers
(who are actually brothers) with such verve and wit that we are ready to
whistle in admiration. Besides, Cal isn't really robbing all those rich
phonies; he's been paid to humiliate the club by Frank DiCilia, who was
blackballed when he applied for membership. When Frank dies suddenly before paying for his revenge, Cal comes to his widow Karen to
collect the debt, not so much for himself but for his accomplices, who

have been jailed and sentenced to 20-to-life for their part in the robbery. Cal himself beat the rap through the talents of a sharp young Jewish lawyer in one of those legal technicalities that Leonard introduces so skillfully. Cal has even been provided a job at Seascape—a Florida dolphin show—just off the Southeast 17th Street Causeway in Miami.

The Seascape episodes of *Gold Coast* rival anything of that kind in recent literature, including the visit to Plymouth Plantation in Penelope Lively's *Moon Tiger,* or the tour of the Edison winter home in Fort Myers in John Updike's *Rabbit at Rest.* Leonard has every nuance, his finger gently pressed on the pulse of Florida as he chronicles the antics of the mammals in and out of the tanks, including Lesley, with whom Cal is soon lackadaisically involved.

When he died, Karen's husband left her in trust of a $4 million fortune to be administered by Dorado Management, a Mafia front, under the secret condition that she never become involved with another man. (This fiduciary chastity belt is a credulity-straining behest, as even the dramatis personae must admit, but we have to take it on faith.) Naturally, the high-spirited Karen rebels against the stricture and learns further that she is being spied on by Roland Crowe, the organization's ruthless enforcer. In a bit of symbolic extravagance, this conscienceless killer is shown mindlessly destroying "several thousand dollars worth of toby jugs and English china" as he chases about Karen's mansion trying to rape her maid (*Gold Coast,* 167). Thus Roland becomes an anti-Roland, the opposite of the Christian knight who strove to save Western culture from the infidel. Cal, on the other hand, though himself a bit of a roustabout, can spot an Asher Durand oil when he sees one (as well as a maiden in distress) and knows the difference between a Louis XVI *bergère* and a Chippendale chair. But he lacks the ambition that convinces Roland he can take over Dorado Management once he has murdered its boss, Ed Grassi. Then Karen and her fortune will fall into his lap, especially because he enjoys the good graces of Jimmy Capotorto, Jimmy the Cap, the capo who will reappear in *Pronto.*

Thus a duel develops between Cal and Roland, as it did between Raymond Cruz and Clement Mansell in *City Primeval.* Karen calls them tussling schoolboys fighting over her. When, for example, Roland, trying to provoke Cal, calls him a "dink," his favorite term of opprobium, and asks Cal who he imagines he is, Cal replies: "Let's see. You wear a range hat and cowboy boots . . . and that suit"—aware of Karen listening—"I'd have to guess you're with the circus"(*Gold Coast,* 178). A sharp tongue, fast left, and a lot of courage are not enough for Karen, however, who concludes that Cal is a "natural-born loser" (208). For his part, Cal begins to think that she is like some dolphins he once freed that returned to captivity when they grew hungry. "They didn't want to be saved. They just wanted to play games" (190).

Duel in the Sun

Split Images (1981) is a hybrid, beginning and ending in Detroit, but with a long Florida interlude. The story is about another duel; this time the cop is Bryan Hurd and the bad guy Robbie Daniels, a spoiled 41-year-old rich boy who murders for thrills. Bryan Hurd was originally supposed to be Raymond Cruz, and *Split Images* a sequel to *City Primeval,* but since ownership rights to that novel were in the hands of United Artists, Leonard was obliged to change Cruz's name and a few others and to make alterations in the story, all of which he did but in such an economical fashion that vestiges of the original remain. Like Raymond, Bryan sports an extravagant mustache and carries his .38 tucked into his pants, with its butt wrapped in rubber bands to keep it from slipping.

Robbie is a villain any reader will love to hate. No longer young but still boyish, he wears soft sweaters over bare skin and often strokes his stomach gently under the fine wool in a gesture of narcissistic complacency. In a first quick chapter, he purposely shoots a Haitian immigrant wandering about his Palm Beach mansion and then hires a broken-down former Detroit detective investigating the shooting for the Palm Beach Police to assist him in the murderous endeavors he envisions in months to come. Like Shakespeare's Iago, Robbie's malignity is motiveless, but also like Iago, he is a victim of pride, seeing himself as superior to others. He is a show-off, not nearly as clever as he thinks, and yet he cannot resist taunting his pursuers, convinced he can outsmart them, forgetting that cops like Bryan are involved every day with criminals. They are the pros, and he an amateur, despite his charm and unlimited financial resources. Insulated from the real world by alarm systems, servants, chauffeurs, exclusive clubs, and walls of all sorts, Robbie has lost touch with the reality that Bryan emphatically has not. Robbie is such a rarified species that he is the subject of Angela Nolan, a photojournalist who specializes in the lifestyles of the rich and not-quite-famous. Her voyeuristic work resembles Leonard's own, letting us peek into the homes of the psychotic rich, as Americans have relished doing since the days of Leopold and Loeb, the Chicago thrill killers of the late thirties.

Robbie, together with Walter Kouza, a right-wing, shots-and-beer, kielbasa-loving homeboy and Florida exile, is going to kill a few social parasites—maybe terrorists, he thinks vaguely—so that he can get to use some of the well-oiled guns in the collection kept locked in his "office." Walter has it in for Bryan, who testified against him in a hearing to determine if Kouza (with eight corpses to his credit already) shot a black kid unjustifiably. In Detroit, Bryan meets Angela and Robbie Daniels for the first time.

In the succeeding pages, Robbie murders three more times, and Bryan begins the chase, aided by Angela, who knows that Robbie "likes to kill people."[4] He concentrates on Walter, now dressed in "Bermudas that covered his knees, new sandals made of straps and buckles and brass rings that couldn't be much lighter than combat boots" (*Split,* 190). Bryan figures that the ex-cop boozer will prove the weak chink in Robbie's armor.

Meanwhile, in his overweening pride, Robbie takes to throwing clues in Bryan's face, once not only displaying the .22 High Standard he used to kill one victim but actually firing it, in the detective's presence, through several glass partitions, taking care to pick up the empty shells with their distinctive marks. This bravado seems pushing his luck a bit, many readers will think. Moreover, even a .22 fired in a confined space will leave the ears ringing, and to find ejected cases is like looking for beads on a broken necklace. But Leonard takes as many risks as Robbie does in this fast-paced story of a plausible madman pursued by a dedicated cop from Detroit to Palm Beach and back several times.

Further, in defiance of all conventions, Leonard allows Angela, a leading figure and by now Bryan's romantic interest, to fall victim to Robbie when she witnesses the shooting of a Porfirio Rubirosa–like character at his mistress's beach house. When Angela sees Chi Chi Fuentes killed, Robbie pursues her through thick underbrush and guns her down while Walter films the event with a camcorder.

The death of Angela late in the story seems risky on Leonard's part, since he has depicted a growing love between her and Bryan with a sensitivity new to his novels of the eighties. As in *Unknown Man # 89,* the lovers withdraw briefly from the fray, although events around them cannot be shut out entirely. Like Frederic Henry and Catherine Barkley in *A Farewell to Arms,* the two seek escape in each other, and as in Hemingway's novel, the woman dies. Whether a film audience, especially in the case of a made-for-TV film, will accept the gratuitous death of the protagonist's sympathetic lover remains to be seen. Even Hemingway experimented a number of times before settling on the present conclusion to his novel. Not until *Maximum Bob,* 10 years later, when Elvin Crowe kills Gary Hammond, would Leonard chance a similar scenario.

Angela and Bryan approach their relationship hardheadedly. Neither is an innocent. Both have been married before and are sexually experienced, and each is reluctant to commit unreservedly. Their discovery of love, made in a series of delicate probes, each reducing the mistrust that both feel, is almost reminiscent of certain seventeenth-century love lyrics, not those of love at that time of year when days grow short (that treatment comes later in *Pronto, Riding the Rap,* and *Out of Sight*) but of the kind that asks: "I wonder, by my troth, what thou and I / Did till we loved?" A vague sense of misgiving arises between the lovers at one point when each wrongly suspects the other has somehow changed, become "different" (*Split,* 213). But her doubts vanish after a brief separation, and Angela resolves joyfully to return to Bryan.

At Angela's death, Bryan goes back to the duel, now motivated by the revenge that so often plays a role in Leonard's fiction. Although Bryan will not defy rules of fairness and decent conduct, he tinkers with them, at one point making sure that the corpse of Robbie's latest victim, Walter Kouza, is discovered inside Detroit city limits. The end of *Split Images* is that of the conventional police story. Ballistics from slugs taken from the body of the Haitian in Palm Beach match those of the bullets that killed Walter; both come from Robbie's .357 Magnum Colt Python. Further, a legally obtained search warrant reveals not only Robbie's Colt but the tape of the shooting of Chi Chi Fuentes he has kept to relive dozens of times. Robbie will not die but will go to jail for many years in one of those hellhole prisons Leonard knows so much about.

Tropical Mischief

Cat Chaser (1982) is a fast-paced thriller set in South Florida and briefly the Dominican Republic, where the greed and passion are elemental, lurking below the idyllic surface of oceanfront houses and hotels, though the endless sunny weather is interrupted when a rainy spell provides a meditative respite for the protagonist George Moran.

In what is often the Leonard mode, the story wanders about in an erratic fashion until settling down and then growing unbearably suspenseful. Typical, too, is the decision to focus on a villain whose original appearance is decidedly unpromising. Jiggs Scully, an ex-cop from New York, is a much cleverer version of Walter Kouza, the rogue cop of *Split*

Images, though equally disheveled. If Leonard had a movie actor in mind, as he so often does when depicting a character, he might have been thinking of someone like Ed Begley: big bellied and bluff, with lots of palaver and a phony smile flashing a full plate of uppers.

The plot of *Cat Chaser* offers an amalgam of *The Moonshine War* and *Gold Coast.* Andres de Boya, like Frank DiCilia, is married to an attractive Catholic girl from Detroit. A former head of Trujillo's Cascos Blancos, the secret police, de Boya even has connections to Dorado Management and the mafioso Jimmy Capotorto. Why Mary Delaney ever married the guy is a mystery, although she provides a limp explanation at one point, just as Karen DiCilia did. The book's similarity to *The Moonshine War* lies in the fact that de Boya has hidden the two million plus dollars everyone wants under the *lit matrimonial,* a big water bed with a special hollowed-out marble base. This cash is insurance in the event that he has to depart suddenly from Coral Gables, as he did from Santiago when assassins cut down his boss Trujillo.

Jiggs Scully, in his shapeless seersucker sport jacket from beneath which a shirttail peeks out, has supposedly been loaned to de Boya by Jimmy Cap to provide the reliable muscle de Boya needs from time to time. Jiggs has his own agenda, however: to get the money he knows is hidden somewhere in de Boya's house. For all his fearsome reputation, de Boya is beset by a variety of problems: his sister constantly besmirches the family escutcheon with her tawdry affairs; his wife Mary takes up with George Moran, another Detroiter who runs a small waterfront motel in Pompano Beach; and George refuses to sell his property to him so that he can build a huge condominium complex on the site. George is a divorced, bearded ex-marine who does things his way, who never fears to speak his mind or march into de Boya's house, where goons once drown a hapless Dominican con man in the swimming pool before our eyes.

George Moran, we learn, had taken part in the 1965 U.S. military incursion into the Dominican Republic. When the book opens, he has decided to return to the island on a sentimental journey to revisit where his platoon (Cat Chaser) saw action, and where he was wounded, and perhaps to find Luci Palma, a girl fighting with the guerrillas the marines encountered. Luci, never seen, is one of the last vestiges of the "native girl" character, the Ingrid Bergman figure, who haunted Leonard for decades. Instead of locating Luci, George meets Mary Delaney de Boya, whom he has always admired, and begins a torrid romance. When Leonard intuits that the Dominican scenes are begin-

ning to flag, he solves the problem by sending the now slightly augmented cast back to Florida, just as he ships them to Detroit in other
books, notably *Out of Sight*. Back in Florida, *Cat Chaser*'s tempo soars,
but none of the host of Latin rascals—including a pair of Cuban brothers in de Boya's employ who specialize in severing the male member
with garden shears—can hold a candle in pure iniquity to Jiggs Scully,
an Irish Catholic who almost made it to Fordham. Scully is determined
that George find out from Mary where her husband stashes his getaway
cash, and when that doesn't work, he's ready to take whatever steps are
necessary to do the job on his own. But George wonders if the robbery
might turn out to be a trick of de Boya's to gauge the depth of his complicity with Mary, or that the treacherous Scully will set him up as a fall
guy for a crime in which he had no part. In any case, the caper concludes
with one of those Leonard switches when close to the end. Mary grabs
the money and escapes from the house—money owed to her anyway
because she has a prenuptial agreement with her husband for $2 mil-
lion. Scully, unaware that Mary has the money, feels obliged to kill de
Boya and his most trusted henchman in one of Leonard's trademark I-
have-to-go-to-the-bathroom scenes. Readers will marvel at Scully's
coolness as he turns the tables on the two men who have just tried to kill
him by firing a volley through the bathroom door. Why he has to shoot
them with a Smith and Wesson equipped with a "hush puppy," a technically advanced silencer, remains a mystery because no need for silence
exists in the remote spot near the Lauderdale airport. Leonard knows
that guns sell books, and they figure prominently in each novel. For *Cat
Chaser,* he also acquired a wealth of information from the Detroit Police
about explosives and about day-to-day activities of private investigators
from Bill Marshall, a private investigator in Florida.

When Scully realizes he's been hoodwinked, he comes after George.
No one handles scenes of waiting for the bad guy to strike and the last
moments of confrontation better than Leonard. Both Mary and George
refuse to compromise by buying Scully off. In a novel full of slippery
Caribbean and ruthless Florida types, the last moments are played out
by three Irish Catholics. George will not run, but he has no intention of
meeting Scully on unequal terms, either. For $200 he buys a .45 from
Nolen Tyner, a broken-down alcoholic detective at the motel, because he
doesn't want Mary to lose what she is owed by her husband. In a few
moments, the trap will be sprung. Somehow the hunter must become
the hunted. And Jiggs Scully is no mean quarry. He only looks like an
oafish blunderer. His arrival is low-key, but in a few minutes he lures

George away from the others for a quiet word before demonstrating the versatility of his hush puppy–equipped Smith. Jiggs is as persuasive as Satan himself: "Something else I got to know. Where'd he keep it? The money. "[5] At exactly the right moment, George picks up the phone and tells his desk clerk to call the police. Jiggs is disappointed. He expected more imagination from George: "There's nothing you can give the cops they can put on me" (Cat, 282). But he has underestimated his opponent. Moran pulls out the .45 from a drawer and blasts him. The police know nothing about the $2 million. He'll take his chances in any investigation into the shooting of a guy with a long rap sheet and a gun in his dead hand. Besides, George will be able to afford a good lawyer.

The brief New York Times review of Cat Chaser called Leonard "better at dialogue than anyone else on the block," making sure that readers unfamiliar with his work realized the book was Leonard's "16th thriller."[6] Jonathan Yardley of the Washington Post also seemed a bit uncertain: "As best I can discover, the tide began to turn for him in 1980." But Yardley concludes after summarizing the story that this new guy in town is "a funny writer . . . and an incisive, unsparing one."[7]

Life after Jail

Stick and LaBrava, both published in 1983, have south Florida settings and take their titles from their protagonists' names. Each teems with the flashy characters Leonard does best: Cubans, snowbirds, ex-cons, yuppies, old-timers, and hustlers of every variety. Both books resound with memories of movies and demonstrate Leonard's extensive knowledge of every aspect of filmmaking.

Stick (1983) is the story of a few weeks in the life of Ernest Stickley of Swag, published seven years earlier. When last seen, he was being arrested at the Detroit airport and went on, we learn, to serve seven years for armed robbery at Jackson State. Now he's out and arrived in Florida, where he hopes to see his teenage daughter and begin a new life. Although he is a resourceful guy, he knows he was lucky to make it through those seven years in one piece. Frank Ryan, arrested with him, was not so fortunate and succumbed to prison rotgut. But Stick hooked up with DeJohn Holmes, who made sure "the hot-shit guys in the wool-knit caps" left Stick alone.[8] The six-foot-four, 240-pound DeJohn took Stick under his wing because Stick had killed "the mother fucker put me in here" (Stick, 52)—Sportree, the bar owner who planned the J. L. Hudson robbery in Swag.

Stick finds a room in a shabby South Beach art deco hotel where the manager sells him a complete wardrobe of comfortable, broken-in casual clothes for $20. Leonard saves further depiction of South Beach, where retirees rub shoulders with Cubano refugees, for *LaBrava*. Stick leaves the beach, just beginning the rebirth that would make it the setting for *The Birdcage* (1996) with Robin Williams, for upscale Bal Harbor, where he works as chauffeur for Barry Stam, an obnoxious wheeler-dealer.

Stick never really settles into one pattern. It begins as a revenge story when Rene Moya, Stick's Puerto Rican buddy from the slammer, now working for drug dealer Chucky Gorman, is shot down handing over payment for a big delivery. But Rainy's death, a case of mistaken identity (but the fault of Chucky), sinks into the background. Much more of *Stick* involves Leonard's interest in moviemaking and the stock market. Several hot tips (Tootsie Roll and MacDonald's) could have earned readers big profits had they invested. But it is how movies come to the screen that gets the most detailed treatment as he explains how independent producers approach slippery investors like Chucky Gorman and Barry Stam to raise money and reveals the dizzying maneuvers that go into tweaking stories and picking casts in a book that George Stade said "gives us as much serious fun per word as anyone around."[9]

In the last third of *Stick,* a schlock film producer named Leo Firestone (the precursor of Harry Zimm in *Get Shorty*) outlines a scheme to profit his investors at the expense of the IRS when they finance his movie *Shuck and Jive*. Kyle McClaren, Chucky's savvy investment counselor, shows him up for the fraud he is while falling for Stick. Kyle, like Angela Nolan of *Split Images,* salutes the feminism of the eighties. From these years on, Leonard's women don't sit around; they produce. Romantic scenes between Stick and Kyle are low-key and always manage to suggest that their relationship must be ephemeral. Wall Street whiz-girls don't often become permanently involved with older ex-convicts.

As so often before, Leonard concocts a double whammy to end his book. Stick manages to con Chucky into putting $72,500 into his bank account for an imaginary revamped version of *Shuck and Jive*. But the last laugh is Mary Lou's, Stick's nag of an ex-wife, who gets a court order to collect from him seven years back child support, just about every nickel he's bilked Chucky for.

Life in Celluloid

LaBrava (1983) is every bit as good as *Stick,* maybe better. It, too, has a large cast (many of whom play walk-on roles), a South Beach setting, and a big dose of film noir nostalgia in the story of Jean Shaw, a screen actress from the golden age of Hollywood's hard-boiled detectives. Joe LaBrava, a former Secret Service agent, has begun a new life as a serious photographer in Miami, a far cry from guarding Bess Truman in Independence, Missouri, as he once did, or sifting through the threatening letters that crazies write to the president of the United States year in, year out. LaBrava—the name everyone uses—is living in another art deco South Beach hotel, the property of a garrulous octogenarian, Maurice Zola, and occupied largely by ancient Jewish females who spend their days observing the sunny street from the hotel's porch, and their nights locked away from the dangers that lurk about.

LaBrava is one of several novels in which Leonard deals with the subject of love and growing old, sometimes humorously as with Cully, the old convict preoccupied with sex in *Bandits;* or with Harry Arno in *Pronto;* and most poignantly with the middle-aged Jack Foley in *Out of Sight.* Still, Leonard is far from ready to employ a protagonist who is the contemporary of Agatha Christie's Miss Marple. LaBrava, for example, is in the prime of his life and tougher than Stick was. When LaBrava encounters a nasty, six-foot-three, 200-pound-plus blond cracker named Richard Nobles who needs attending to early in the book, he fires off his camera's flash in the guy's face and lays him out on the floor in short order. Pulling Nobles's .357 Smith and Wesson from his waistband, LaBrava sticks the barrel into his mouth and says: "Suck it. It'll calm you down."[10]

But nothing calms down Richard Nobles who is involved with Jean Shaw. Jean awakens unlimited devotion and admiration in LaBrava and Maury Zola. She represents at once Leonard's salute to the magic of movies—and movie stars—and to the "eternal female." Jean Shaw is an icon of an earlier age, a woman who lifts boys to manhood and reduces men to boys. She appeared in 16 films before LaBrava was out of his teens, always playing a femme fatale whose simmering sexuality in movies like *Nightshade, Deadfall,* and *Obituary* made her far more desirable than her wholesome rivals. Here Leonard tinkers very slightly with chronology, since he invents at least a half-dozen movies with earmarks of the years 1945 to 1955, when LaBrava would have been not much more than 10 years old.[11] Now splendidly preserved at age 50, Jean Shaw keeps falling into dialogue from her old movies, and when she plots the book's caper based on her films, she becomes for a moment Leonard himself doing pretty much the same thing. Jean's slightly wacky idea is to extort $60,000 from Maury Zola with the assistance of Richie Nobles, and to use the sum to pay Zola back the money he has lent her in recent years. Paying back her debt with money stolen from the lender not only makes no sense but requires that Richie be eliminated from a share, a decision requiring his liquidation. That little task Jean manages at the end by plugging the expendable country boy with her Walther PPK.

Because Richie was such a horrible human being, most readers will be as ready to forgive the raven-tressed vamp as LaBrava. The rest of her plan turns out to be pretty harmless, though it causes the Miami police countless hours of overtime and results through no fault of Jean's in the shooting death by his Cuban confederate of Richie's old snuff-chewing, homeboy uncle.

Jean Shaw's larcenous scheme germinates from a dozen or so of her old movies plus the rejected screenplay she once wrote for Harry Cohn about a woman who cons an agreeable playboy out of his money just so she can pay her own way. As smitten as he is with her, LaBrava still figures out her game in short order with the uncanny detecting skill shared by detectives and nondetectives in Leonard's stories. As the end approaches, he says: "They found Richard." Jean replies coolly: "There is no way anyone can prove I killed him." Whammo. He's got her. "I didn't even say he was dead," LaBrava says (*LaBrava,* 231).

Their romantic relationship is complicated by his knowledge of her shady character, but more provocatively by the fact that Leonard identifies with them both, making their union faintly incestuous. Like Jean Shaw, Leonard has derived a generous income from Hollywood and has used movies to inspire his books. Like LaBrava, he loves movies passionately and looks to them for insights. In addition, like LaBrava (or Stick and others), Leonard unconsciously regards himself as a small guy who takes on the big ones year after year.[12] Both lovers are aware of the roles they play, LaBrava to such an extent that he asks himself how he is to measure this momentous event, taking Jean Shaw to bed: "It wasn't something he would tell anyone. He would never do that. Though it seemed like the kind of thing you might tell a stranger on a train without naming names. On a *train*? Come on. He was making an old-time movie out of it" (*LaBrava,* 87).

For real sex, we are referred to Franny Kaufman, the free-spirited *maedl* who sells Mary Kay–like cosmetics to the old Jewish women on the porch of the Della Robbia. Her spiel shows that Leonard pays closer attention to infomercials than most TV viewers. But Franny's role in the novel is peripheral, and she does not appear to have a permanent claim on LaBrava's affections.

In *LaBrava,* Leonard continues to show a sensitivity for individual scenes as they will appear on the screen. The visual image and the language go hand in hand as when LaBrava bravely meets Richie Nobles in a Miami park at night. It's *mano a mano* again, and again the smaller guy evens the odds by quick-witted improvisation lest brute force triumph. In this case, a baseball bat lessens the handicap. As in their first encounter, LaBrava is able to knock Richie down and once more stick a gun in his mouth, "feeling he should tell him, 'I think you're in the wrong line of work' " (*LaBrava,* 186). Readers will revel in Leonard's deadpan "feeling he should tell him," but moviegoers will eventually love the fast action and the "wrong line of work" retort. Both might ask themselves, however, if LaBrava could count on finding a bat in the dark at the right moment.

The next five novels abandon Florida, but starting in 1991, Leonard returned with a vengeance, publishing another five in a row set in southern Florida, all of them among his best.

Mermaids and Murder

Maximum Bob (1991) is without question one of Leonard's finest, a richly textured book drawing on a number of disparate pop sources and bringing together a wide variety of characters from across the social scale. As American sensitivities heightened in the late eighties toward instances of bias and prejudice previously tolerated, newspapers reported stories of judges around the country whose intolerant racial and gender remarks had heretofore been dismissed as judicial humor. At a time when hackles were being raised in many jurisdictions about prejudice in the courtroom, Leonard was introduced coincidentally to a Florida circuit court judge named Marvin Mounts whose antics color *Maximum Bob,* but not to such an extent that Mounts took offense at the book or at Leonard's dedication of it to him. The womanizing Bob Gibbs is a composite figure, being the same height and age (at the time) as Leonard and looking like Leonard's favorite film personality, Harry Dean Stanton. Bob Isom Gibbs, known as "Big" on his election posters and to his wife, is an obnoxious little tyrant whom Leonard comes to like better as the book progresses. But for much of the story, he has about as much patience for the diminutive bigot who thinks he's funny as Gilbert and Sullivan did for their "judicial humorist" in *The Mikado.* Like him, Bob Gibbs seems to be a candidate for an early execution. When we first see him, a hanging judge who "has put more offenders on death row than any judge in the state," he is handing down a maximum sentence to Dale Crowe Junior, a vacuous parole violator and scion to the Crowe clan, a family of white-trash losers right out of an abnormal psychology textbook.[13]

When Leonard found himself losing interest in Dale Crowe Junior ("I didn't see an important part for him in the book," the author says innocently on a BBC video), he switched focus away from him to his uncle Elvin Crowe, who emerges as one of Leonard's all-time nastiest bad guys.[14] Fresh out of state prison at Starke, Elvin's experiences there serve to remind us what a total bust the correctional system is. Elvin and Dale Crowe Junior share the same parole officer, Kathy Diaz Baker, a no-nonsense second-generation Cuban American with one bad marriage behind her. Leonard was surprised to find that the majority of Palm Beach parole officers were women, and since he was trying to get away from another cop protagonist, and his wife Joan was urging him to create female characters who were more assertive and career minded, he seized on Kathy.

Maximum Bob depicts a brash, rapidly changing Florida, a melting pot where Cuban Americans are often more observant of traditional American values than old-timers like the Crowes. Florida is a place where men and women wear lightweight summer suits but pack guns, where the alligator is still a powerful totem, and where the unseen spirit world intrudes on the commercial realities of tourism and electioneering.

Bob Gibbs married a "mermaid" at the popular Weeki Wachee water show whose near escape from a gator during her act convinced her that she is in psychic contact with a 12-year-old black girl killed by just such an amphibian more than a century ago. To document passages dealing with out-of-body experiences and warnings from the Great Beyond, Leonard used materials he and Gregg Sutter had accumulated about spiritualists from upstate New York who founded the town of Cassadaga, Florida, early in the century. This research, including visits to mediums of both the old school and the flashier new Florida variety, would serve him again in depicting Dawn Navarro, the psychic in *Riding the Rap*.

Bob Gibbs is getting tired of his wife, Leanne, whose growing inattention to her diet displeases him almost as much as her spiritualist concerns, which he sees as a liability to his political life with its numerous social functions. He yearns to replace her with a younger, svelter model like Kathy Baker. Bob's scheme to achieve this end provides a subplot to the novel and brings him into unknowing contact with Elvin Crowe, who kills for pleasure and profit. Elvin has been hired in a rather unlikely arrangement to off the judge by Dr. Tommy Vasco, a drug-using dermatologist whose license has been revoked. Elvin is a twenti-eth-century grotesque, a towering anthropoid in an electric-blue suit smelling of mothballs, from a contemporary Florida subculture whose every idea and notion is a twisted parody of reality—and one of Leonard's scariest and most fascinating psychopaths.

Of course, Elvin is bone stupid despite his conviction that he is smarter than everyone else, "the kind of guy thinks he knows everything and can beat the system," as Kathy puts it. His jail time was spent for shooting the wrong man in a roadside rest area, something he regards as an honest mistake. Although he has some of the best lines in the book, he exhibits all the bad guy signs. He talks too much, for one thing, and he's a slob for another, because in his fiction, Leonard associates order and cleanliness with decency and mental health as did Hemingway, who was not nearly as tidy as the compulsive Leonard (whose spotless desk and habit of making deadlines with weeks to spare testify to his pen-chant for order). His Elvin Crowe, living amid empty bottles and pizza cartons, and sleeping in a bed that a crackhead prostitute finds dirty, is a long way from the wholesome personal habits of Ernest Stickley and Raymond Cruz.

Leonard delays the appearance of Elvin's opponent, Gary Hammond, until *Maximum Bob* is a third underway, but once there, he begins relent-lessly bird-dogging Elvin, who is gunning for Judge Gibbs. The fates of all concerned are soon interwoven as the judge attempts to shed his wife with the assistance of a gator-poaching in-law of Elvin's while seeking to attract Kathy Baker. Gary Hammond, meanwhile, has not only figured out Bob Gibbs's scheme but is on to Elvin Crowe and his connection to Dr. Tommy Vasco. Elvin's antecedents may go back to Marshal Ferris Britton of *Killshot* and the cocky Richard Nobles of *LaBrava,* but he remains one of a kind, a character to chill the blood.

Only the lovers, Kathy Baker and Gary Hammond (a melding of a new America with an older one), show any love and trust. Like Bryan Hurd and Angela Nolan, they explore their new love, joyfully discover-ing that it is real. While the others betray each other in endless permu-tations and live in dysfunctional relationships (like Dr. Tommy Vasco with his homosexual houseboy Hector, or philandering Bob Gibbs with his gentle mermaid) that parody the real thing, Kathy and Gary move to genuine fulfillment.

As in *Split Images,* Leonard tests the limits of popular fiction when Elvin shoots Gary Hammond as he has his hair cut. Further, the death of this attractive character is gratuitous in that it advances no worthy cause. In fact, this scene stands in contrast to the opening scene of *The Bounty Hunters* (which Elvin partially read in prison) when Dave Flynn, having his hair cut in a Western town, forces the villain Frank Rellis to back down.

The finale of *Maximum Bob* sees the death of Elvin at the hand of Kathy and Bob's wife, Leanne, who has been apprised of Elvin's evil presence by her familiar, the little black girl from beyond the bourne. In a nod to *Gunsights* and to the role of women in the eighties and nineties, women carry out the job that the men failed to do. The world will be a better place without Elvin Crowe.

Jail or Bail

Every bit as good as *Maximum Bob* is Leonard's next, *Rum Punch* (1992), a sequel of sorts to *The Switch*. At least Ordell Robbie and Louis Gara are back, the two "fuckups," as Melanie calls them—she's back, too.[15] Like *The Switch*, *Rum Punch* is a three-card monte with shopping bags of money rapidly changing hands before our eyes amid a spate of killings, at least six.

Leonard tells two stories simultaneously. The first is about Ordell, now running guns, which he buys or steals assisted by "jackboys,"" wild black teenagers so strung out on drugs that they have almost as little regard for their own lives as they do for the lives of others. The second unfolds the relationship between two middle-aged lovers, he approaching 60, she in her mid-forties.

Jackie Brown, the movie version of the book, concentrated on her, changing her name and the color of her skin, thus adding an extra handicap to the problematic romance. In Quentin Tarantino's film, Pam Grier (as Jackie Brown) plays the role of a black Jackie Burke, a three-time loser at the altar and a stewardess on a two-bit airline who is making a last effort to turn her life around and start over, almost as if she had just found a Chinese cookie that promised "Love and Fortune await you soon."

The "fortune" part will depend on her ripping off Ordell, for whom she acts as a courier, bringing bundles of cash into Florida from Freeport on her frequent Bahamas flights. This risky enterprise occurs to her when she is stopped by two cops tipped off by an informant about her errands. The nature of the caper identifies her as gutsy but tainted, an independent woman making it in a man's world by bending the rules. How much we are never quite sure; nor is Max Cherry, a Florida bail bondsman who falls for her.

Max is largely based on Mike Sandy, a West Palm Beach bondsman, even to possessing that gent's pump action 12-gauge Mossberg with a laser sight, but he has a speck of Leonard in him, too. Of slightly French ancestry from Louisiana, with a chameleon name, Max is not your average bail bondsman. For one thing, he's pretty honest; for another, he's more sensitive and observant than most of the breed. He treats his shifty clientele with a respect they often gratefully reciprocate. Rounding up a skinny Puerto Rican kid the office calls Zorro for his romantic pretensions, Max not only shares drinks with him at his house but graciously puts away a "big soup plate of *asopao de pollo*" served up by Zorro's mother (*Rum Punch,* 65). Sitting in the young burglar's run-down living room, Max tolerantly regards the boy's taste in interior decoration: "Bullfight swords in leather scabbards crossed beneath the Sacred Heart of Jesus. There were other mail-order swords on the walls, sabers, a cutlass, a scimitar, several pictures of the Blessed Mother, St. Joseph, different saints; Max recognized one as St. Sebastian, pierced with arrows" (65).

Max reads poetry once in a while and, of course, knows his movies—and his movie queens—cold. But neither his business nor his private life is running smoothly. The Mob has infiltrated Glades Mutual in Miami, the insurance company Max deals with, and he has been living apart from his wife Renee, currently the patron of a no-talent young Cuban painter in her no-profit art gallery at the mall for which Max pays the rent as well as all her other expenses. Florida is changing. The South Miami Beach depicted in *LaBrava,* where "old retired people from New York sat on the hotel porches wearing white hats, their noses painted white, and boat-lift Cubans worked their hustles down the street" has begun to gentrify, as even that dim bulb Louis Gara notes (*Rum Punch,* 101). But those ubiquitous bail offices and pawn shops that shock the northern eye are still there, as are the gun stores. South Florida has now become the gun capital of the world, where cheap guns are made or assembled and imported for sale throughout the United States or are exported legally or illegally to trouble spots like Colombia.

Ordell's Jamaican jackboy Beaumont Livingston has been picked up on a weapons charge, and Ordell wants to bail him out before the previously convicted offender can make a deal with the cops to reduce charges; but he is too late. Beaumont has already revealed that Ordell regularly gets cash earned by his gun business brought in from the Bahamas by Jackie Burke, an Islands Air flight attendant.

Now Ordell is really feeling frazzled. He kills Beaumont and arranges with Max Cherry for a second bail for Jackie, who has been caught at the airport bringing an undeclared ten grand into the United States. But he still worries that Jackie might talk just as Beaumont did, and all this is happening on the eve of a big caper he's been planning for weeks. Back in *The Switch,* Ordell learned that neo-Nazis like Richard Monk were into guns, and he has managed to hook up with one in Palm Beach who has a huge arsenal of exotic weaponry by feigning sympathy with the looney's theories of racial separatism.

Ordell is counting on stealing Big Guy's collection of military hardware from his survivalist outpost in the boonies and shipping it off to eager customers from one of the smaller Keys where a former fisherman from Jamaica waits with a boat. But Ordell must be dead certain that Jackie keeps her mouth shut, and that his passel of jackboys, recruited for the gun operation ("rum punch") doesn't blow the whole thing with their reckless behavior. It's enough to make a dude's head spin.

However, his old partner, Louis Gara from Detroit, just out of the slammer for the third time, may be willing to lend a hand. What Ordell doesn't realize is that Louis's last stretch seems to have permanently boiled his brains. While he still looks like a take-charge, hard-assed guy, Louis has become a zombie, unable to function on the outside.

The ingredients of this witches' brew are all brought plausibly together with perhaps the slight exception of Louis Gara, whom the mob has shortsightedly placed in Max's bail office to keep an eye on things and provide some muscle. *Rum Punch* seems living proof of Leonard's dictum that the right characters with the right names will make their own story.

Jackie's nicely documented night in a women's prison brings her into contact with Max Cherry and convinces her it is time she parted company with Ordell—not without some monetary compensation, however. Jackie is another in the line of Leonard's ambiguous noir heroines like Karen DiCilia and Jean Shaw. Her aggression, understated rhetoric, and endless appetite for cigarettes identify her as an oral personality who seeks reassurance in Max's love—after she convinces him he should assist her in the switcheroo she plans for the final curtain, when she will grab a half a mil from Ordell under the eyes of the Feds. Like Andre

Dubus, whom he admires, Leonard finds women smoking sexy; and like Jackie Burke, who gets Max Cherry back on cigarettes in short order, Leonard's own appetite for tobacco returns each time he tangles with a new mistress, each time he gets into another book.

Jackie's ambiguous need for Max makes her no pushover, however. On the contrary, she'll take him only on her terms. She is a self-reliant nineties woman who can reach into a man's glove compartment one moment to grab his Airweight .38 and use it to threaten another's crotch within the hour:

> "I believe that's a gun pressing against my bone."
> Jackie said, "You're right. You want to lose it or let go of me?" (*Rum Punch,* 116)

Rum Punch offers several satisfying shoot-outs before the last one when Ordell gets his, including one between 50 or more cops and Sweatman, Snow, and Zulu. The three jackboys are handicapped by their inability to read the simple instructions on the handheld rocket launcher they had counted on using against the fuzz. As AFT agent Ray Nicolet says disgustedly: "Couldn't read it, could you? You dumb fuck . . . You should never've dropped out of high school" (*Rum Punch,* 275).

On the last page, Jackie, unlike Karen DiCilia, invites Max to come along with her on a voyage of discovery in the "borrowed" black Mercedes of the recently deceased Ordell. (Max wonders understandably if you can "borrow" a car from a corpse.) He's probably going to accept the offer. It looks like "love and fortune" did come to Jackie after all.

Old Guys

Both *Pronto* (1993) and *Riding the Rap* (1995) feature Harry Arno, a protean figure whose antecedents lie in his predecessors Al Rosen and Maury Zola, all of whom seem vaguely Jewish—although only Rosen actually proclaims some Jewish ancestry. Loosely based on old-time Hollywood movers and shakers whom Leonard encountered, these characters also contain doses of organized-crime figures and a touch of Leonard himself. They bear little resemblance to the few characters of the books identified as Jewish, mostly men, like Marshall Fine, who gets Cal Maguire off the hook in *Gold Coast;* or Jay Walt, the repo man of *Unknown Man # 89;* or Barry Stam, the know-it-all yuppie associate of Chucky Gorman in *Stick.* Rather, these are senior citizens fighting the aging process but still able to hold their own against the competition in a tough world, guys who remind us of Bugsy Siegel or Meyer Lansky but who are beginning to slip. Their names, their backgrounds, even their ages and their hair are subject to revision when necessary. Now, as they grow older, they are starting to become touchy, crotchety, even tiresome, insisting on reviewing the past for younger girlfriends and associates who have limited tolerance for such nostalgia.

Leonard loves these characters and understands them and sneaks into their characterizations his own personal qualities and idiosyncrasies, but he grows impatient with them, just as those around them do. They are show-offs who want attention. Maurice Zola, with Leonard-like recall, insists on reciting "every stop on the Florida East Coast line from Jacksonville to Key Largo" (*LaBrava,* 58). Zola alone was born in Florida, but Harry Arno feels at home there, and Al Rosen seems to be trying to turn Tel Aviv into Miami Beach. All three look backward in time and place.

Harry, the bookie, eats at Wolfie's (but no pastrami since his angioplasty) and remembers South Beach before it went downhill, let alone before it began to go upscale. Once he flees the beach for Rapallo, Italy, a step ahead of Jimmy Capotorto's chief goon, Tomasino Ritonto, the Zip, Harry becomes so annoying that Leonard allows him to sink into the background to concentrate on the contest between Raylan Givens and the Sicilian hitman.

Kidnapping, Florida Style

In *Riding the Rap,* Harry's role is so minor that the reader has little time to grow weary of him. On the contrary, his motor mouth and solipsistic attitude win grudging approval. Ignoring the violent nature of his kidnappers, and as blind to the danger of his circumstances as Mr. Magoo—even when another of their victims is shot to death in his presence—Harry continues to regard his captors with more contempt than fear.

But the heart of the story is devoted to Raylan Givens and the Florida present. Harry has become an anachronism like Maurice Zola before him, who watched "swamps become cities" and whom he vaguely remembers: "Changes were no longer events in his life. They had happened or they didn't."[16]

Riding the Rap shows its Western antecedents to those who look closely. Raylan Givens is a Western hero of cool nerve and split-second reflexes, capable of Natty Bumppo–like accuracy with his 9 mm and as able to outthink his Puerto Rican and Bahamian foes as Ross Corsen could the Mescalero Apache Bonito in an *Argosy* story back in 1953.[17]

If Dawn Navarro, the psychic, is no "freckled, clear-eyed"[18] Katie or Joyce Patton (formerly Joy, the topless dancer) either, other things haven't changed much: marijuana for tulapei, and closed-circuit TV for keen eyesight. But the renegade breeds and the white crooks are still present danger. Florida has become a kind of high-tech Arizona with everything moving faster, and Leonard keeps up with pages of hip, crisp dialogue and sentence fragments when they are needed.

Riding the Rap is vintage Leonard, a good story where the laconic Westerner—Raylan comes from no farther west than Kentucky—faces not one but two villains in addition to their hapless boss, the decadent rich boy Chip Ganz. Of course, the marshal is more detective than cowboy, but even in the first scene, we're back to *3:10 to Yuma* as Givens transports none other than Dale Crowe Junior from Ocala police custody back to Palm Beach County. When Dale starts to whine about the injustices he's suffered, Raylan allows (as Randolph Scott might have), "If you're gonna talk I'll put you in the trunk" (*Riding,* 3). Dale has to learn to ride the rap. Don't do the crime if you can't do the time.

Better and Better

Leonard's next novel, *Out of Sight* (1996), is even better. At first glance, it seems as if he's going to serve up *Stick* again: a basically decent guy gets out of prison after many years and finds himself on the gold coast and attracted to a woman who reciprocates his feelings. But Ernest Stickley was released, whereas Jack Foley breaks out in one of the coolest and funniest episodes Leonard has ever written.

What lifts *Out of Sight* figuratively out of sight is its gently elegiac tone. Jack Foley, less wooden than Raylan Givens, is 47 going on 100, and his luck in discovering Karen Sisco fills him with an awe he communicates to the reader. The fairy-tale quality that sometimes sneaks into Leonard's gritty, realistic stories strikes the right key. It seems fitting that only part of the story is set in Florida, which, though tough and cruel, is still the sun-splashed source of the fountain of youth. After Foley "flees" (a word he notes is best relegated to newspaper accounts) the state for Detroit, the whole world becomes dark, cold, and snowy, death's second self. In *Out of Sight,* Leonard seems to be asking us the same question Robert Frost once did: which way do you want to go, fire or ice?

Chapter Five
Leonard's Worldview

How "serious" a writer he is is a question that sometimes bothers Leonard. Although he often dismisses his prolific achievement in one breath as storytelling and entertainment, in another he grows mildly defensive that he can be accused of failing to deepen a reader's awareness of life. To what extent he has fulfilled that obligation remains to be judged, but what he has to say is clear. No one can write 35 novels without imparting a view of life.

To begin with, it is wrong to expect total consistency from him. Leonard's major contribution to American literature is well-written, gripping crime fiction. He is not the proponent of a philosophical system. He began by writing superior though fairly conventional Westerns. In his 1999 *Be Cool,* synthetic background music becomes an issue of contention. When "Trail of the Apache" was published in 1951, neither rock and roll nor electronic music existed. For many years, Hemingway's pessimistic ethos influenced Leonard's thought as much as did the earlier writer's terse dialogue and restrained prose style. Today little of that bleak vision remains.

Leonard insists that his own voice is not to be found in his fiction, asserts that the reader must never be aware of the author, and claims that his characters' thoughts and views must not be seen as his. We need not take him too literally, however, since his objectivity is no greater than that of other writers in the naturalistic-realistic tradition, all of whom have shown a partiality for one character over another, for one opinion over another. Thoughtful reading of his books and consideration of his wide popularity reveal that not only does he promulgate a worldview but that it is one acceptable to a mass audience.

Optimism and Pessimism

Leonard's beliefs differ little from those of most Americans. Raised a Catholic and sympathetic to the teachings of the church in its less restrictive and authoritarian forms, he has grafted on to his Catholicism the largely Emersonian optimism and trust in self-reliance that has become the unofficial doctrine of the United States despite two world wars and the Holocaust. A worldview that relegates the existence of evil to a peripheral role might seem an anomaly in one whose stock in trade involves violence, murder, and betrayal. But it is an inconsistency by no means unusual in American life. Leonard's personally cheerful outlook resembles that of Ronald Reagan—another "Dutch"—whom Leonard cordially detested for his insensitivity on social issues and human rights, and whose foreign policies he excoriated in *Bandits*. Both men tend to interpret life in terms of movie episodes and film personalities—life imitates art—and share the conviction that the forces of evil don't stand a chance in the long run.

In Leonard's eyes there is something too melodramatic about absolute evil. To his generation, it was personified by Hitler, the great enemy. A figure to seize the imagination with his piercing eyes, hysterical voice, and talent for pageantry, Hitler was also faintly ridiculous—too much of a bad thing. Some of the early books feature monsters like Frank Renda, whose labor camp at Five Shadows reflects the concentration camps of the Third Reich, but Leonard's later Nazis (such as the pathetic Richard Monk of *The Switch* and Big Guy, the biker in *Rum Punch*) earn only our derision. Francis X. Perez—like Hitler a renegade Catholic—is drawn at first as a figure of monumental evil but has so mellowed by the conclusion of *Unknown Man # 89* that he is ready to offer the protagonist Jack Ryan a job.

Stupidity

In the last century, Emerson convinced America that evil is a negative quality, the absence of good. Just as there can be nothing completely cold, for some heat can be measured in it, so there can be no absolute evil. It appears only when good is lacking. For Leonard, evil is usually an intellectual deficiency brought about by pride, for which he accords as healthy a respect as any church father. His identification of evil with stupidity grows from one novel to another until in *Be Cool* Chili Palmer expresses the belief: "You get into crime you have to be kinda dumb," (289).

All Leonard's criminals are "kinda dumb," but each is convinced he's smart. They have no self-control. They talk too much and listen too little. They are impulsive and impetuous, distracted by any novelty. Richie Nix is a case study of what educators call attention deficit disorder. While his sidekick Armand Degas is explaining to him what they must do to avoid arrest, "Richie was stabbing the knife at the kitchen counter trying to hit a crack in the vinyl surface" (*Killshot*, 125). Harry Arno's pretentious allusions to Ezra Pound, "a very dear friend of mine," cause his kidnapper Louis Lewis to ask his boss, "Who's Ezra Pound?" The brains of the operation replies: "He was a heavyweight. Beat Joe Louis for the crown and lost it to Marciano" (*Riding,* 86).

Comic Visions: Subcultures

Leonard is a master of several kinds of comic writing but depends chiefly on depicting how a subculture attempts to adopt the norms of those it perceives as its "betters." Often it is blacks who no longer attempt to arrange their affairs "just like the white folks" (as they did in racist American humor for more than two centuries) but more likely emulate a sorry pattern of their own race than, say, a Mafia model. Whether they are black, white, or Hispanic, they are inevitably at the bottom of the social scale. Leonard writes almost exclusively about the lower and lower middle classes. Thus criminals like Raji in *Be Cool,* Bobby Shy, Elvin Crowe, or Ordell Robbie set goals that are parodies of others. Richie Nix seeks the distinction of holding up a bank in every state, and Roland Crowe longs to take control of Dorado Management (a Mafia enterprise) by killing its current boss. Leonard's carefully restrained point of view serves to accentuate their misguided behavior. Their wrongheaded approach to every undertaking underlies the essence of his humor. Because their values are so stupidly askew, their lives are zany carica-tures of what they should be. A case in point is the murderous and mud-dleheaded Elvin Crowe of the Florida Crowe clan, whose history recalls classic naturalistic theories of heredity. Elvin disapproves of drugs: "Why go to all the trouble to buy that shit, have to deal with niggers mostly, when you could get all the beer and whiskey you wanted driving no more than two blocks in any direction?" (*Bob,* 177). Evil in the abstract—as opposed to stupidity—is a Manichaean vestige, now the exclusive property of nutcases like August Murray, who leads the Gray Army of the Holy Ghost in *Touch* and thinks he is Ignatius of Loyola.

Dialects

A stratified society offers the writer skilled in the resources of language and rhetoric (as few crime writers are) the opportunity to resort to dialect and low speech, and Leonard never misses the chance. For one who speaks no other language but his own, he has as sensitive an ear for various patois as he does for dialogue in general, a "Panasonic ear."

He captures black speech as few writers since Mark Twain have, catching its lyric quality, its volubility, and its streetwise cadences unfailingly. He resorts to words he finds repeated in court testimony and police statements, such as "man," "shit," and "niggers" (or "nigga"), or phrases like "how you doing." He drops auxiliary verbs and articles and employs the figurative language he himself avoids as well as colorful vulgarisms. Ordell Robbie's running commentary on a white power march in Palm Beach opening *Rum Punch* provides an illustration:

> Young skinhead Nazis. . . . Look even little Nazigirls marching down Worth Avenue. You believe it? Coming now you have the Klan. Some in green, must be the coneheads' new spring shade. Behind them it looks like some Bikers for Racism, better known as the Dixie Knights. We gonna move on ahead. . . .
>
> Man, all the photographers, TV cameras. This shit is big news, has everybody over here to see it. Otherwise, Sunday, what you have mostly are rich ladies come out with their little doggies to make wee-wee. I mean the doggies, not the ladies. . . . How you doing, baby? You making it all right? (1, 2)

Leonard's Latin speech is more restrained than his black English, more solemn, as if each Cuban, Puerto Rican, Dominican, or Nicaraguan carries the sorrow of the Aztec and the pride of the Hidalgo at the tip of his tongue. But it is linguistically haphazard. Leonard ignores the difficulty that Spanish speakers of English have with the initial *s* or with *y* and the English *i*. Nor does he attempt to translate Spanish idioms and construction into English (as Hemingway often does), though he will insert an occasional Spanish word or a *como se dice*. He frequently drops the *d* or *ed* of the English past tense to give the effect that we are hearing a Spanish speaker, and he will often make use of a formal "yes" or a rhetorical "of course" to achieve the same effect. For the most part, he merely suggests Spanish: "Of course, why not?"

Of more prolonged comic effect is the sharp satire he habitually leveled beginning in the seventies at large and small absurdities of American life. A perceptive observer possessed of a wry sense of humor, he is given to pointing out the disparity between what is and what should be without calling attention to his efforts. The objects of his derision range widely, from spoiled celebrities accustomed to the gratification of every whim to a criminal justice system distinguished for its failures: "It was an unwritten rule in Hollywood, actors never ordered straight from the menu; they'd think of something they had to have that wasn't on it, or they'd tell exactly how they wanted the entree prepared the way their mother back in Queens used to fix it" (*Get Shorty,* 319). Elvin Crowe offers avuncular advice to Dale Crowe Junior on how best to "ride the rap" in *Maximum Bob:* "You poke or get poked" (50). Once there was a time, he concedes to his nephew, before convicts were "inmates," when things were different; but now "all they think about is getting dope and getting laid. . . . get salty quick as you can. . . . you're a new punk coming in. . . . The first one comes at you and you back down, you're pussy. What you have to do is boo him up. A nigger, you have to stick him" (108).

Satire

Touch and *Bandits,* published in 1987 though written almost a decade apart, provide illustrations of sustained religious and political satire. In *Touch,* Leonard displays a fascination with religious fundamentalism, a lifelong interest that attracts him as it did Mark Twain, Sinclair Lewis, and Erskine Caldwell. Rascally preachers have lost little of their allure for Americans even as the century draws to a close. If anything, television has increased their presence. But Leonard is more concerned with the environment that breeds them. August Murray is neither a clergyman nor a Protestant nor out to line his pockets. Rather, he is a fanatic representing one extreme of religious experience. *Touch* deals with the same themes that captured Euripides in *The Bacchae,* the age-old conflict between the new and old, between inspiration, mysticism, spontaneity, and individualism and formalism, ritual, tradition, and authoritarianism.

August Murray, another man of diminutive stature and delusions of grandeur like *Get Shorty*'s Michael Weir, combines the behavior of a soldier with skills of a computer nerd. First seen in a courtroom of Detroit's Frank Murphy Hall of Justice charged with assault and battery, he stands in brown shoes, feet exactly 18 inches apart, ready to do combat. His breast pocket stuffed with pens and lined with a plastic pocket saver, he is prepared to defend his faith—or his version of it—with the talents of a Jesuitical apologist.

The leader of OUTRAGE (Organization Unifying Traditional Rites As God Expects) has been arrested for interrupting mass to hand out pamphlets. But his tongue is sharp in his defense: "It didn't look like a mass to

me. . . . Guitars, tambourines, I thought maybe it was a square dance."[1]
Leonard carefully avoids creating a paper tiger. Murray scores points in
the courtroom as often as Hermann Goering did at Nuremberg, and like
the Nazi, Murray questions the authority of the court, demanding the
judge disqualify himself as "excommunicated from the Church . . . following your recent divorce and . . . remarriage" (*Touch,* 43).

Free Will

Often regarded as rigidly deterministic, writing unsentimental accounts
of marginal human beings in a world they never made, Leonard is actually the contrary, believing like Jack Delaney in *Bandits* in personal
responsibility: "I did it to myself. The intellect presents it [an action].
And the will says no way or let's do it."[2] But this sort of strictly orthodox Catholic doctrine presented in parochial school terms does not mean
that Leonard is a dogmatist. Lucy Nichols, the former nun who serves as
his *raisonneur* in *Bandits* (as Juvenal did in *Touch*) rejects any savor of formalism. Leonard's best clergy (often former clergy), like Chaucer's,
teach through their lives, work directly with the faithful, and exude a
Christlike charisma.

Lucy Nichols serves at Carville, a leprosy hospital that Leonard had
visited as a boy with his maternal uncles, the Rivé brothers, who
repaired the organ there. Lepers (victims of Hansen's disease) represent
in several books for him the most wretched of God's people, those most
needing the "touch" of the servants of Christ.

Lucy's father, a wealthy oilman his wife calls "Texas Crude," represents the lip service Catholic and mindless defender of the church. Pos-
ing as hale-fellow-well-met, his every move is shrewdly calculated. On a
visit to Lucy in Nicaragua, he won't shake hands with the staff at the
leprosarium for fear of contagion or meet disfigured patients but writes
out a check to the hospital for $100,000.

Committed to anticommunism, Dick Nichols supports the Contras
in Nicaragua, whom he regards as a bastion of democracy and Christian
civilization, including the murderous Col. Dagoberto Godoy, a particularly vicious Somoza alumnus. Armed with a letter of recommendation
from Ronald Reagan and CIA assistance and entrées arranged by Dick
Nichols to wealthy businessmen, Col. Godoy is touring "the Pelican
State" to raise funds.[3] Needless to say, he has no intention of taking the
$5 million he collects back to Central America, and Jack Delaney's felo-
nious associates have every intention of assisting him in that endeavor.

Slapstick

Slapstick humor plays only a small part in most stories, though Leonard does not reject it entirely. A senior citizen's search for sex leading to a rest home weaves its way through several chapters of *Bandits,* and *Gunsights* presents Phil Sundeen's attack on Dana Moon's forces as a circuslike spectacle attracting the likes of showman Billy Washington.

The Moonshine War, five years later, contains many of the same elements as *Gunsights.* Westernlike, set in Prohibition era Kentucky, it too concludes with a disastrous attack and features another duo, often antagonistic, who team up to defeat the bad guys. Son Martin, the protagonist, resembles Jack Ryan of *The Big Bounce* more than Jack Delaney or Roberto Valdez or John Russell of the Westerns that bracket *The Moonshine War.* Technically outside the law as a liquor distiller and possessed of a short temper, Son wins the reader's approval for his courage, toughness, and trust in his instinct. He never backs down in a confrontation, even against enormous odds. But unlike later heroes such as Chili Palmer, for example, Son's humorlessness and proclivity for incredible feats link him to the less sophisticated early books that lack Leonard's irony and comic touch. Here the situational comedy often depends on broad figures: the country sheriff, the floozy, the fat crook with flashing dentures whose superficial bonhomie hides depths of malevolence.

Skirting outright caricature, the novel draws on popular notions of folkloric figures such as hillbillies and "revenooers" that conjure up memories of the slapstick and black humor of Erskine Caldwell's *Tobacco Road* and *God's Little Acre,* both of which Leonard had read, with their venal sheriffs, allusions to buried wealth, and bleak depictions of rural Americans in the worst years of the Great Depression.[4]

Son Martin has been bequeathed by his father 150 valuable barrels "of top grade moonshine" that lie hidden somewhere on his farm (just as gold is supposedly to be found on Ty Ty Walden's place in *God's Little Acre*). With his faithful black retainer Aaron (like Ty Ty's Uncle Felix), Son Martin will defend his territory against a treacherous army buddy who is now a federal agent and the help the traitor recruits. This includes a former dentist turned big-time bootlegger, his young female "secretary," and Dual Meaders, a psychotic who ruthlessly enforces his boss's will when not indulging his own sadistic inclinations. One of these is to force a helpless café patron to strip naked and hand over his suit and gratuitously force the man's wife to do the same, perhaps

Leonard's vague memory of Will Thompson's shocking disrobing of Griselda in *God's Little Acre*.

Jewish Characters

Because he rejects evil in the abstract and Original Sin as a Christian construct, Leonard has grown progressively fonder of certain Jewish figures (particularly his "could-be" Jews) whom he admires as enterprising and less susceptible to the sin of stupidity—though their advantage as concerns pride does not seem markedly greater than that of others. Further they are often equipped with varieties of what he objectively (and impatiently) sees as his own weaknesses. But since his visit to Israel and his deeper involvement with Hollywood, sympathetic Jewish characters, now often women such as Frannie Kaufman or Elaine Levin, have appeared more frequently.

Changing Character

According free will an important place in his ethic, despite frequent charges of nihilism, Leonard sees great latitude for change existing in human lives. He is convinced that AA altered his outlook and behavior permanently and believes that others are equally capable of change. Being nonjudgmental and tolerant of human weakness, he often draws characters who become more (or infrequently less) sympathetic as a story progresses.

In this respect, he avoids creating characters who are simply flattering idealizations of the reader or flat characters who change at a moment's notice, long the bane of much popular fiction. Verne Kidston, the implacable enemy of Paul Cable, comes to like him in the final pages of *Last Stand at Saber River*, and Bob Rogers Jr. and Jack Ryan bury the hatchet when they both see they have nothing against each other; but Frank Long does them one better when he goes from friendly toward Son Martin to antagonistic and then back to friendly.

Right and Wrong

In Leonard's cosmogony, Eve's acceptance of the serpent's blandishments would not be wrong because she disobeyed God with all his rules but stupid because she was flattered into listening to a not terribly convincing snake. The punishment for being stupid is more stupidity and seems to be what God provided humanity after the Fall. Leonard's God, who remains backstage, is an ironic Jewish deity with an antipathy to stupidity. He created human beings with free will. People know what's right and wrong. Leonard's admirable characters strive to do the right thing. In doing so, they are true to that voice within them, the traditional conscience more than Emerson's voice of God, but it amounts to the same thing. Thus Leonard's view of human nature and morality is comfortingly orthodox. But while he is always tolerant—like a good liberal—he does not believe for a moment that people are the victims of society. Rather, society is the victim of people.

The Leonard Hero

The decent guy (or gal) listens to his conscience and does what he's supposed to. Thus self-reliance achieves a significance only a little less than Emerson's God reliance. A Gary Hammond or Raylan Givens may bend the rules from time to time. But being antiauthoritarian does not mean there are no rules, just fewer, maybe two or three fewer than those Moses brought down off the mountain. Leonard's self-reliant protagonists, usually male but now also women, are true to their self-imposed codes. They have usually grown up Catholic and have a divorce behind them, the fault of the other partner who was more materialistic and pretentious. They are growing alienated from the world around them and in danger of cultivating eccentric habits but keep their moorings via contacts with their dads or a few levelheaded colleagues—often black—on the job.

Chris Mankowski, the bomb squad cop of *Freaky Deaky,* displays the typical qualities and shares this worldview as well. From a blue-collar background, Chris is not quite anti-intellectual, being only 10 credits short of a college degree. But because he relies on feeling and intuition, he tends to be suspicious of formal education and intellectuals. Such folks are exemplified by the excessively literal psychiatrist who examines Chris and even Robin Abbott, the manipulative villainness of the book, who writes romance novels "with a lot of rape and adverbs" in them and reads Charles Bukowski and Genet (*Freaky,* 205).

Chris's powers of deduction rival those of Poe's Dupin, however, when he begins to put the pieces together to solve a crime ("suppose Skip was here, working on that movie" [*Freaky,* 87]). His presence of mind equals the Western heroes' proficiency with a six-gun. In an attempt to locate Skip Gibb, Chris phones Robin and identifies himself as Skip. She hangs up. But a moment later, her phone is busy, revealing that she's calling Skip to say what just happened, and telling him Skip is in town.

Such heroes are streetsmart, too. Chris knows in advance exactly how lawyers will discredit Greta Wyatt if her rape charge against Woody Ricks reaches the courtroom. He can spot Donnell Lewis from five feet off: "Where'd you do your time, Jackson?" (*Freaky,* 87). But he is charitable and wary enough not to push the black man beyond the point both recognize as suitable for a tough white cop. Having felt him out, Chris allows Donnell to maintain self-respect.

Leonard knows, like Emerson, that "character is higher than intellect," but his leading figures are never dummies. They are perfectly attuned to their time and place, knowledgeable about movies, popular music, celebrities, and TV—from all of which they manage to form opinions and make shrewd judgments, moral, psychological, and aesthetic. Chili Palmer renders a dangerous opponent helpless by taking a cue from a Clint Eastwood movie; Vincent Mora, whose command of the American music scene rivals a record executive's, measures the appointments of an upscale hotel by the technology of *Star Trek*.

Calvin Maguire knows his more prominent French, English, and American antiques and can instantly spot a Hudson River canvas, but he has gained his expertise in the breaking-and-entering field. Typical is the performance of Carmen Colson. When she and her husband watch *Jeopardy,* "Carmen would get more right than Wayne" (*Killshot,* 89). He manages to triumph over her only when the question is about two adjacent states whose names mean "red" in Spanish and Indian. Wayne wins that one (Colorado and Oklahoma) because he had been hunting there once.

Women

Carmen Colson modestly defers to her husband most of the time, but she is clearly brighter than he and just as gutsy. Leonard's women have grown much less submissive in later books, a trend he once attributed to the influence of his second wife, Joan, but one that seems inevitable. Like many of the post–World War I generation of American writers he had read, Leonard finds a good deal edifying in the struggle of women to achieve equality and their renewed activity in the seventies, and it inspired him to create a different woman than he had previously. Many readers will find these characters not altogether successful, however, since Leonard continues to measure them largely in men's terms and by male standards.

Like his men, his women characters are unattached, now no longer mistresses, wives, or dependents. As new careers opened to women, they became cops, lawyers, stockbrokers, probation officers, and federal marshals. But sharing men's work and their habits are not the same. Mickey Dawson busts loose of stifling Bloomfield Hills domesticity like Ibsen's Nora, but the scenes of her drinking and smoking weed with lowlifes Ordell Robbie and Louis Gara in *The Switch* don't seem so much liberating as unlikely.

Until Karen Sisco and *Out of Sight*, Leonard seems a tad uncomfortable about showing his women bibulous or pugilistically inclined. Jean Shaw may end up in the drunk tank at South County Mental Health, and she is capable of drilling a guy if need be, but she does not tussle with him. Karen, on the other hand, uses a folding steel baton to repel Kenneth's advances, whipping him upside the head without batting an eyelash. Although a suitable birthday gift from her dad may be a Sig Sauer 9 mm, she gives clothes a lot of thought, too, and worries what being locked up in a car trunk with a muddy escaped convict will do to her Chanel suit. They may all be liberated women, but they are still depicted as sexy and erotic. Levelheaded, maternal Joyce Patton is a former topless dancer. Many of them are attracted to outlaw guys despite their taste in expensive shoes. Kyle McClaren of *Stick* pulled in more than a hundred grand a year back in the early eighties, but she finds herself smitten by a jailbird; and Carolyn Wilder learns after a beating from Clement Mansell that her highfalutin civil libertarian notions must give way to the practicality of Detroit dick Raymond Cruz.

The Victorian contrast between the "tainted" or "bitchy" woman and her more "pure" or "feminine" cousin, surfacing in so many of the books, fades in the latest ones: *Cuba Libre, Out of Sight, Riding the Rap,* and *Pronto* contain no such conventional dramatic pairings. In *Out of Sight,* Jack Foley's ex, Adele, is such a good-natured paragon that it's hard to say why he finds Karen more attractive. Moreover, Adele didn't shoot her last two boyfriends.

The delicate restraint displayed in Leonard's cautiously erotic love scenes, and the uncertainty and fear of being hurt exhibited by both men and women, alleviate any lingering doubts that his female characters are only projections of male desire. Good sex is shown as consensual between equals, unlike the exploitative brand a score or more bad guys practice. Leonard's heroes and heroines are sensual beings, to be sure,

but they are not condemned for being so. Unlike those who do everything in excess, the sympathetic figures control their emotions and savor
their sensations; yet the pleasures the good and the bad enjoy are the
same. Thus alcohol, sex, and soft drugs—marijuana but no acid or
heroin—are indulged in, but for the good characters, they are seen as
rewards to be enjoyed when work is done.

Duty

For Leonard, of course, work must be socially constructive, yet that definition is broad. Harry Arno's bookmaking activities provide a service
but require mastery of quantities of arcane lore and strenuous days. Like
Faust, Leonard feels that work liberates the spirit. No idle monasticism
for this Jesuit product who maintains a rigorous morning-to-night writing schedule with no lunch break and makes as much demand on his
characters as on himself, though he concedes in several novels, "if it ain't
fun, it ain't worth doing." His greatest contempt is reserved for lazy
mountains of flesh like Woody Ricks, who spends his days in an alcoholic haze and floats in his indoor pool listening to show tunes; or Robbie, the homicidal sybarite who auctions off to foreign buyers the heavy
machinery of the business his father built; or Chip Ganz, sponging off
his senile mother in a rest home, looking for runaway teenage girls at
Dreber Park in West Palm Beach where the Huggers gather. In his early
fifties, Chip tries to get the parents of these kids looking for the love
generation they missed to send him money for their safe return.

Past Lives

In the earliest novels, sympathetic protagonists tend to possess clean
pasts: no misdeeds cloud their lives, though they may have been
unjustly accused of crimes, as Corey Bowen is of rustling cattle in *Escape
from Five Shadows*. Not until we meet Jack Ryan in *The Big Bounce* do we
encounter someone who has not only strayed outside the law but who
continues to. Later, main figures tend to have put their criminal tenden-
cies behind them if they ever possessed them. Ernest Stickley specializes
in armed robbery in *Swag* but reforms admirably in the sequel, *Stick*.
Leonard seems of two minds about this sort of lawbreaking: first, it is
usually minor, a gesture of protest against a self-righteous society, or at
least a learning experience; and second, it belongs only to a transitional

phase in the character's life. The perpetrator with more maturity turns away on his own from the life he has led.

In the first Chili Palmer book, *Get Shorty,* Chili is the object of curiosity about his previous gangster connections and his career as a shylock. Although he does not exactly justify his calling, he explains that he always warned customers of the risks they were about to undertake and that he never found violence necessary. Indeed, he insists that injuring a debtor made repayment more difficult and was bad for business. Asked by Harry Zimm if he has ever been arrested, Chili says: "I've been picked up a few times. They'd try to get me on loan-sharking, or a RICO violation . . . but I was never convicted, I'm clean."[5] Although his answer is slightly evasive, he clearly intends to put his old life behind him and to begin a new one, making movies. His *vita nuova,* he finds (to readers' delight), proves not greatly different from his old one when it comes to the people he meets. Chili Palmer, like Old Blue Eyes whom he admires, is a proponent of that American brand of self-reliance called rugged individualism, and it serves him well. Only in *Be Cool,* the sequel to *Get Shorty,* do we learn that his runaway success *Get Leo* was followed by a box office disaster, *Get Lost,* when he allowed himself—against his better judgment—to do the bidding of Hollywood insiders. The moral is crystalline: Go it alone.

Virtues

Whatever their pasts, Leonard's protagonists are men and women of courage and initiative, braver than we are and possessed of magnetism and charisma that command the respect of others. Often they face multiple opponents or, more likely, a single foe (as is the case in *City Primeval, Gold Coast,* and *Glitz*) in situations and settings that seem pedestrian enough but are unlike any we will ever face. Their opponents have usually done hard time in prison. Sometimes they are out to get the man they hold responsible for their incarceration. Teddy Magyk stalks Vincent Mora in *Glitz,* looking for a chance to revenge himself on the cop who arrested him more than seven years ago. Like the others, he is an overreacher and show-off, a spiritual son of Poe's Montressor in "The Cask of Amontillado," believing like him that a "wrong" is imperfectly revenged "when the avenger fails to make himself felt as such to him who has done the wrong." But when Teddy first makes his presence known to the detective, he finds that Mora has forgotten him "because all of you shifty ex-con assholes look alike."[6]

In addition to combatting Teddy, who seems always aided by a law that favors criminals (a bit of right-wing sentiment the liberal Leonard absorbed permanently from his police contacts), Mora finds time to neutralize Ricky Catalina. Here again he marches in where angels fear to tread. Convinced correctly that Ricky may have information about the murder of a Puerto Rican prostitute, Mora approaches him head-on while the brutal enforcer is making his weekly rounds collecting protection money. Not only does Mora rough up the tough guy with "the dead stare," but he convinces the gangster that he's a hit man sent from Miami to rub him out (*Glitz*, 130).

The Hunted is much more conventional in the courageous acts performed by the marine sergeant David Davis, who fights off a passel of crooks out to get Al Rosen in Israel, just as the language and sentiments are more Hemingway: "He went with the black one to a cafe, then the black one left," or "The Laromme's the best hotel in Eilat . . . you can get lost looking for the discotheque, but it's a lot of fun."[7] But as he grew more experienced, Leonard learned that little gestures require courage too: daring to go into an alley, agreeing to meet someone untrustworthy, entering a hotel room that might be occupied, or slipping into a house at night as Chili Palmer does. When ex-marine George Moran goes along with two unsavory characters to Andres deBoya's Florida mansion in *Cat Chaser* or meets with Jiggs Scully, he is taking a risk as great as Davis in leading a firefight from an isolated desert house near Wadi Shlomo.

While David Davis has the earmarks of the less subtle figures of books before *Unknown Man # 89* and *City Primeval*, he differs from them in being less of a loner. In *Hombre*, the book most closely resembling *The Hunted*, John Russell ignores the plight of a former soldier being bullied out of his stagecoach ticket. Russell must be cajoled into leading the group of passengers left stranded after the coach holdup. David Davis is more social and more amenable. But both guide their little groups through similar mishaps, crossing deserts, keeping the money out of the bad guys' hands, hoping they can rely on men who fail them at the critical moment, conducting parleys from the buildings they defend, and always remaining faithful to the others, even when they show no gratitude. John Russell becomes a mythic figure in his sacrificial death: "You will never see another like him as long as you live" (*Hombre*, 190). When the smoke clears, Davis may take the loot for himself because no survivor has a better claim. But both are men of utter loyalty amid the treachery that surrounds them.

Vices

Undoubtedly it is Leonard's obsession with the other side of loyalty—betrayal—and with dysfunction that relates his worldview most closely to the noir. Every novel offers illustrations. In *Pronto,* Nicky Testa's shooting of Jimmy Capotorto before their scheduled visit to Butterfly World is a betrayal, but so are Harry's withholding a portion of his bookie take and Jimmy's contract on Harry's life, in turn based on a deliberate FBI leak that Harry is stealing from him. For its part, the FBI is sacrificing Harry to obtain a conviction of Jimmy while Jimmy's girlfriend Gloria is unfaithful to him with both Nicky and a Sicilian hit man with ambitions of taking over Jimmy's Miami operation. These sexual shenanigans, like Jean Shaw's relations with three men in *LaBrava,* harken back to classic film noir as much as does the complicated plot. There women with roving eyes are usually identified as nymphomaniacs and often drug addicts as well. Lauren Bacall's dysfunctional sister in the *The Big Sleep* (1946), Chandler's novel with screenplay by Faulkner, is both.

Dysfunction

In Dashiell Hammett's *The Maltese Falcon* (1930), which made a star of Humphrey Bogart, betrayal goes wholesale. Today Leonard finds the film amusing for its labored exposition, but it made a lifelong impression on him, even to his paraphrasing in *Stick* Bogart's line to Sydney Greenstreet about a "crippled newsie" taking Elisha Cook Jr.'s guns away from him.[8]

In this most famous of Hollywood hard-guy detective stories of the forties, the *ménage à quatre* led by Caspar Gutman (Sydney Greenstreet) is so perfidious it is difficult to keep track of their treachery. Nor are they slouches when it comes to dysfunction, exhibitions of every sort found in the noir catalog from outré sex to child and substance abuse. Leonard's dysfunctional characters indulge in equally varied activities, but he depicts with special relish their bizarre social relationships: many are between women and their abusive husbands or boyfriends, guys like Frank Renda, Virgil Royal, Clement Mansell, and Snoopy Miller. Others occur between homicidal young men and middle-aged women, themselves no models of mental stability. Involved in such are crackpots like Richie Nix, a killer and ex-con living with 50-year-old Donna Mulry, who worked for more than a quarter of a century in prison kitchens. Or

Richard Nobles, a dangerous good old boy and part-time security guard involved with Jeanie Breen (aka Jean Shaw), a onetime minor Hollywood luminary. Also a security guard is the neo-Nazi Richard Monk, who lives alone since his wife ran off with their child, in a house in a working-class Detroit neighborhood, the home still redolent of his dead mother's graceless presence. Teddy Magyk, too, lives with his mother, whom he is on the verge of killing, and we witness him murder an old woman met in an Atlantic City casino. After a bout of necrophilia, he stuffs her corpse beneath the boardwalk.

In an age when writers trip over each other trying to be more "pop," the noir label has become honorific. At once it connects an author drawing on crime subjects to a ready-made tradition stretching back to the likes of Chandler and Hammett, to say nothing of Robert Mitchum, Barbara Stanwyck, Ray Milland, and Bogey. Clancy Sigal typically extends his blessing in a 1987 review of *Bandits* in the *Listener,* beginning: "Leonard . . . possibly owes his largest debt . . . to Forties *film noir.*"[9]

Noir and Modernism

Although the origins of noir are still in dispute (the role of Jacobean tragedy, Poe, German expressionism, and other disparate elements being allotted different measure according to various formulas), there is no question that the movement is an outgrowth of the early-twentieth-century modernism that suffused Western literature before and after World War I with cynicism about all political, religious, and social structures. The pessimistic sensibilities of noir are those of modernism filtered down to a popular level via those huge influences on Leonard, the movies and the pulps.

Often appearing in popular sources later than in belles lettres, noir endured longer as well. But Leonard knew both modernism and noir for he had read some Eliot, Joyce, and Pound as well as seen films like *The Big Sleep* and *The Blue Dahlia* (1946). In fact, it is difficult even for the expert to distinguish the noir from the modernist when we consider that Faulkner's modernist manifesto *The Sound and the Fury* (1929) was published the year of Hammett's noir classic *Red Harvest,* or that Faulkner's 1931 "potboiler" *Sanctuary* has often been called both modernist and noir without arousing scholarly objection.

Leonard's extensive firsthand familiarity with noir is best displayed in *LaBrava,* where he exhibits encyclopedic knowledge of the genre even to the creation of a movie actress who played in a series of invented films from that bygone era.

How well he knows Eliot and Joyce is open to question. Leonard certainly knew Hemingway, and not just *For Whom the Bell Tolls,* which he had practically memorized, but earlier novels, too, as well as *Across the River and into the Trees.* Facetiously Leonard makes Harry Arno of *Pronto* (a figure with whom he slightly identifies) a devotee of the modernist poet Ezra Pound, though the reader suspects, along with Harry's girlfriend, the Miami bookie has little understanding of the master's verse. But a fondness for complexity and unresolved endings and for sudden starts that suggest a debt to the modernist aesthetic (like his partiality for outsiders and his awareness of lost coherence) may owe as much to movies and paperbacks as to *Prufrock* and *The Waste Land.*

Leonard may snort when the word *noir* surfaces, but he has thoroughly imbibed its aura. He hired a researcher, Gregg Sutter, who once envisioned a magazine dedicated to American crime fiction to be called *Noir.* Moreover, Leonard (with Sue Grafton and Donald Westlake) engineered the successful nomination of Mickey Spillane to Grand Master in the Mystery Writers of America. (Leonard has never lost his admiration for the octogenarian, whose brutal stories set in a McCarthyist world of confusion and betrayal are the last flowering of the noir in American detective fiction.)

Leonard's trust in social organization is limited. The cops are usually straight, but prison is a colossal failure in a country with more per capita in the slammer than in any other industrial nation. And the church is mostly a distant memory. His morality, nonetheless, is strictly conventional. Adam Begley, in the *New York Observer,* is on the money: "Personal responsibility . . . is the lesson Mr. Leonard wants to share."[10] That doesn't mean even the good guys say no all the time to sex and drugs, for these pleasures can be well-earned rewards in the computer age.

In modern fashion—if not modernist—Leonard delights in bringing diverse areas of experience together, in presenting the shocking and unsettling, and in drawing his experience from popular sources. He begins his stories arbitrarily—it's the "second act," the second hundred pages, you have to worry about, he says. He frequently shifts point of view, returning consistently to one or two figures. In praise of Quentin Tarantino's way of letting characters create a scene and tell a story, Leonard says: "In *Pulp Fiction,* these two guys are going to kill somebody and they are talking about what you call a Quarter Pounder with cheese in Paris—a Royale with cheese. And that's what I do."[11]

It is truer than Leonard likes to think that his books are heavy with the elements of noir: slippery people, dangerous cities, sleazy hotels, restless cops, violence and corruption, and the stolen money; what Nicholas Christopher calls "the lifeblood of the city . . . necessarily a central issue in all *noir* films."[12] But only in his depiction of betrayal and dysfunction does Leonard tread the strict party line.

His delicious sense of humor is something the noir crowd could never approach. Although he gives us a slimy world, none of his stories are imbued with that enveloping darkness and nihilism that reduces human beings to victims. Leonard is no prophet of doom. The paranoia and hopelessness that characterize Cornell Woolrich are not there. The reader always knows who the bad guys are and who did it. No one in these books stands up in an abandoned brewery like Peter Lorre in Fritz Lang's *M* and declares, "Ich kann mir nicht helfen" [I can't help myself].

Chapter Six

"Dope, Sex, and Rock and Roll": Pop Strains and Formulaic Elements

Is It Literature?

Because Leonard has become a perennial best-seller, it is tempting to regard his output as mass production and his readers as consumers. But production alone cannot negatively determine a writer's status. Both John Updike and Joyce Carol Oates have published copiously without seriously inviting that charge. To link prolificacy with lack of merit implies criteria not yet established. Nevertheless it seems clear that an enormous readership involves satisfying demands somehow less fastidious than—if not hostile to—those of a select one. Consideration of Leonard's work from such a perspective may teach us something about the nature of popular fiction.

This century has established as a critical axiom the notion that all fiction falls into two large categories: serious and commercial. Although these categories are nebulous, they describe writing that can usually be recognized when it is encountered, difficult as it may be to define. That such definitions remain unsatisfactory is reflected in the fact that the terms "serious" and "commercial" are not universally used, and that others such as "interpretive" and "escapist" or "popular" seem equally valid—or invalid.

How long ago was that golden age when a social and intellectual elite enjoyed the same literature as one below it? In heroic society, all listened with equal pleasure and edification to the bard's epic song, we are told. That climate changed, and eventually some literary efforts began to be regarded as "light," "low," or "trivial," a process that roughly paralleled the rise of the novel itself and the growth of the middle class. Technical innovations such as the steam press hastened the division, but as late as the turn of the century in America, certain men of letters, notably the "schoolroom poets" Longfellow, Lowell, and Holmes, enjoyed the recognition of all classes of readers and the blessings of public education as well. Today, of course, these poets are read by neither the top nor the bottom.

Two generations ago, critics liked to point out that Hemingway and Fitzgerald enjoyed both critical and popular success. The waitress or beautician was as fond of Papa's love stories as the academic poking about in his chronicles of the Lost Generation's disillusionment, written in a prose eschewing subordinate clauses. At one time, Fitzgerald appeared in the *Saturday Evening Post,* as Leonard would, available on the table in the dentist's office or the barbershop. Many will recall, too, the invariably futile attempts of more imaginative high school English teachers to assure classes that Shakespeare began as a popular playwright and was not always the icon of high culture he has become.

If any lesson emerges from all of this, it is that no clear-cut distinction exists between serious and escapist fiction. Many books are hybrids. The great distinction always invoked—that a lesser literature seeks solely to entertain whereas a more serious one looks deeper into our lives and ourselves to make us better understand the human condition—is certainly not without validity, but it is always highly hypothetical. Leonard travels comfortably back and forth across the invisible and shifting border between popular and serious fiction, never lingering too long in one spot. His own considerable uncertainty as to where he belongs has in its way contributed to his success. He is at home in both camps.

The popular writer is inevitably accused of serving Mammon, of writing for the buck. Leonard started writing by the word for the pulps, the most commercial market available at the time. He has always been paid for his writing, but it is also a labor he performs willingly, and he is totally honest when he calls money just a way of keeping score. Lucrative contracts assure him that he can compete, that there is demand for his work. At this stage in his life, he would probably write for nothing because, as he says, it is what he does; it's fun. He feels that his imaginative powers are stronger than ever, and the closest thing to writer's block he suffers is the uneasy feeling between books that he ought to get started on the next one immediately.

Like most writers, like virtuosos of any field, he can belittle his accomplishment on occasion; but there is a note of bravado when he does, as if the gods must never learn how much he really cares. Even then, he doesn't so much denigrate his work as dismiss its import, asserting a breezy disinvolvement, a limited interest in the setting and period of his Westerns, for example, or a dismissive admission of how often he has written to order at top speed. But these remarks are made in the same spirit as Fitzgerald's to Hemingway about how he could at any time dash off a story to fit *Post* requirements. More indicative of Leonard's true feelings is his often repeated assertion that early movie sales supported him as a novelist.

Naturalism

By choice and inclination, Leonard writes loosely in the familiar tradition of naturalism and realism, having little patience with postmodernism (or metafiction) and the experimental. Like the "Dirty Realists" he so admires (Raymond Carver, Russell Banks, and Andre Dubus), Leonard has a powerful sense of place. Like them, too, he writes about the working class. What Patrick Meanor says about the figures of "trailer park fiction" applies equally to Leonard's: "The protagonists have lives that are rootless, poverty-ridden, and empty. Early marriages end in divorce and are riddled with alcoholism, abuse and other self-destructive behavior. . . . The alienation and brutality that these writers portray are sometimes more disturbing than the generalized cosmic dread and nihilism of Kafka and Beckett because the downtrodden characters live in 'Edenic' America."[1]

But Leonard takes great liberties with the naturalistic tradition when it suits him. As a naturalist, he generally maintains a detached view of life and portrays the commonplace with great accuracy. His documentation has become even more fully realized since *Glitz*. Not in the least obtrusively, Leonard handles esoteric subjects such as psychic readings and the promotion of rock groups with the kind of detail found in extended *New Yorker*–like magazine articles. Of course, situations in which physical confrontations, guns, and killings take place are not the quotidian experiences of most readers, but neither are they so remote that they stretch credibility.

He avoids the propagandistic commitment to the downtrodden of so many naturalists because he believes in personal responsibility and free will, but his sympathy is clearly with the underdog, with Mexicans, Nicaraguans, reservation-bound Apaches, and Cuban peons, as well as waiters who serve movie stars, families at the mercy of the repo man, and guys who need a second chance. Nor does Leonard see environment as unfailingly shaping the individual though his most memorable villains are born into circumstances that restrict their development. His awareness of heredity, while not classically naturalistic, surfaces in his choice of characters like the felonious Crowe family or Bryan Hurd, Kyle McClaren, Jack Delaney, Kathy Diaz Baker, and Karen Sisco, guys and gals from decent families—especially with decent dads.

A rogues' gallery of psychotics and sociopaths, "characters of marked animal or neurotic nature," as Vernon Parrington long ago identified them, shows another strong naturalistic influence. But a deterministic outlook, with its concomitant pessimism, is absent in Leonard's world-view. Thus his "naturalism" must be called eclectic, sharing many of the salient features of that durable philosophy but rejecting its most promi-nent one.

Plot

Although Leonard's novels regularly win him comments such as "well . . . plotted" and "plot is intriguingly mystifying," he tends to pooh-pooh plots himself, insisting in romantic fashion that plots write them-selves if the characters are right.[2] Most critics don't see it that way. David Lehman, writing in *Newsweek,* called the thriller *Glitz* "an insom-niac's dream," stressing the indisputable truth that Leonard's books are suspenseful page-turners.[3] At any rate, his plots are always lineal, although he often introduces characters whose early promise doesn't come to much, or women whose existence serves only to provide a pro-tagonist with a choice, a device he has carried over from the Westerns.

Leonard relies heavily on suspense because his books involve a central conflict that is violent, physical, and ongoing. *Glitz* may keep several stories bubbling at once, but the central one is the conflict between Teddy Magyk and Vincent Mora, a conflict not of ideas but of action. When Teddy comes to shoot Mora in his hotel room, and the detective somehow discerns his malevolent presence at the door, the encounter ends in gunfire, not spirited discussion.

Likewise, *Stick* and *Out of Sight,* both of which start as the stories of decent guys just out of prison, soon focus on a primitive conflict between the central character and a primary antagonist who wants to kill him. Essentially, then, the crime novels are episodic and heavily dependent on plots fired by basic conflicts resolvable only by physical clashes. The nature of the crime thriller demands a large measure of vio-lence, action, and moral simplicity. To compensate, Leonard minimizes his violence by making the scenes brief, though frequent enough to stimulate. The reader may wait impatiently for a killing to come in *Cat*

Chaser, but when Jiggs Scully murders General deBoya and his hench-man Corky, the deed is done in one detailed but bloodless paragraph.

Just as Leonard attempts in plotting to avoid the simplistic motiva-tion that provides conflict in much popular fiction, he avoids its pre-dictable happy endings through a variety of devices. For example, when lovers come together, it is seldom understood that their relationship will endure. *Split Images* and *Maximum Bob* witness the deaths of major fig-ures, whose lovers must continue without them. In *Gold Coast,* Karen diCilia blows the hero off in a rather unsatisfactory conclusion to an oth-erwise dandy thriller. In *Out of Sight,* federal marshal Karen Sisco shoots her erstwhile lover Jack Foley, who is taking part in a house invasion (though she does not kill him as he asks), then recovers sufficiently by the next morning to tell her father casually: "He knew what he was doing," to which he replies with calculated understatement in the book's last line, "My little girl . . . the tough babe."[4]

Hollywood, finding that ending insensitive, had Jack driven off to prison in a van with a savvy black convict played by Samuel L. Jackson (making a lighthearted cameo appearance from *Pulp Fiction* and *Jackie Brown*), hinting that the two men wouldn't remain long in captivity.

Because for the reader of popular fiction, the plot is the story, and the story the book, plots filled with dangerous encounters, escapes, and gunfire figure prominently, and Leonard does not fail to deliver these. His plots are richly detailed and appear seamless, though such perfec-tion is often an illusion. Would the suspicious Ordell Robbie of *Rum Punch* trust Cedric Walker of Freeport with his money to the extent he does? Would the Mafia consider for a moment the services of a redneck cracker of questionable mental health like Roland Crowe? In the same novel *(Gold Coast),* Dorado Management goes to endless and illicit trou-ble to carry out Frank diCilia's capricious demand that his wife never become involved with a man after his death. It is one thing to restrict a financial settlement to a young widow who remarries, but quite another to order her social life restricted *in perpetuam* by intimidating potential suitors. Even odder is the elaborate scheme Jeanie Breen (aka Jean Shaw) concocts to victimize Maurice Zola in *LaBrava* when he is already willing to give her anything she wants.

The conventions of the thriller call for a revelation of the criminals (murderers) and their being brought to justice. Leonard is able to avoid the first condition because their identity is never a secret, but he must accede to the second in every book. Out of a horror for predictability and pat endings, his conclusions are often left indeterminate or are "tricky"—not quite the same as "trick," which he associates with O. Henry and shoddy writing. Rather, Leonard considers such endings ironic, offering powerful evidence that the universe is moral: in the words of Ralph Waldo Emerson, "Commit a crime, and the world is made of glass." The really bad guys almost always die, and the good guy may get the girl or just go back to being alone. Often, sympathetic figures (as well as those less so) find the rug pulled out from under them: Ernest Stickley will not get the money in *Stick* (nor did he get it in *Swag*). Jack Delaney gets nothing, either, and like Cal Maguire and Chili Palmer ends up pretty much back where he started.

Characters

Reviewers find little to complain about in Leonard's plots but wax even more lyrical over his characters: "They reinvent themselves all the time using whatever materials come along."[5] His characters reflect the belief that Leonard has been spelling out in interviews for years, one that he lets Chili Palmer explain in *Be Cool:* "I don't think of a plot and then put characters in it. I start with different characters and see where they take me."[6]

Chili himself is a case in point, Leonard would argue. Born in Brooklyn, Chili moved on to Miami, where he shylocked for the Mob until on a hunt for a welsher, he came to California and stumbled into the movie business. A guy who always lands on his feet, he works a trade that evokes horror while still managing to be the sort of fellow everyone respects. Men as well as women admire him, but he takes nothing from anyone. At the end of *Get Shorty,* he apparently blows his big chance in films by telling an obnoxious movie star that the big shot is all wrong for the shylock role he covets in Chili's projected movie: "You're too short" (*Get Shorty,* 357). But Chili's courage is as long as his patience is short. In *Be Cool,* when Linda Moon shows reluctance to stand up to her manager, a young black hood named Raji, Chili's question to her, "You want me to speak to him?" says it all (46).

Leonard's main characters may have faults, but they are the kind we can live with. They are the guys we want to be: tough nonconformists who do things their way. Told in a posh Beverly Hills eatery that his suit and tie betray a lack of self-confidence, that in the entertainment business "you don't give a shit how you look, your talent speaks for itself," Chili runs his gaze around the place and says, "So where should I get my clothes, the Salvation Army?" (*Be Cool,* 7). To quote Emerson again: "Wherever MacDonald sits, there is the head of the table."

The characters of these stories belong for the most part to popular or escapist fiction, with the usual yawning gap between the good guys and the really bad ones. But early and late, Leonard manages to come up with a number of in-betweens and always a host of walk-ons who stay in our minds. Many, both major and minor, are roughly modeled on movie stars, from his days of Gary Cooper and Randolph Scott right up to Harry Dean Stanton and Steve Buscemi. Others are bits and pieces of Hollywood types; Jean Shaw, for instance, owes to Jane Greer and Barbara Stanwyck. They find themselves involved in situations more dramatic than ours. They pack guns, kill, and come in contact with people living lives we just read about.

Often they resemble each other to an uncanny extent. Jack Foley, Jack Delaney, Jack Ryan, and Ernest Stickley are not the same man, but neither is one completely distinct from another. They differ largely in their degree of toughness: Jack Ryan, Vincent Majestyk, and George Moran are number 10s, and Jack Delaney, Jack Foley, and even Chili Palmer lag behind at no more than 8 plus. The psychos share resemblances, too, varying mostly in how colorful they are, or being distinguished by their attire (cowboy hats, smelly blue suits). Sometimes they favor a characteristic remark like Clement Mansell's all-purpose derogatory adjective "chicken-fat" or Roland Crowe's dismissive substantive "dink"—in the spirit of that other popular writer of genius Charles Dickens with his "Barkis-is-willin'."

Fortunately for his readers, Leonard's villains are so compelling. Unlike Dr. Moriarty whom Sherlock Holmes pursues, they are not generalized figures but spastic jumping jacks whose grotesqueness holds our fascinated attention. If we seek to identify with Leonard's heroes, we distance ourselves from these anthropoids whose behavioral aberrations demonstrate how dimly they grasp values others accept. These whites, blacks, and Hispanics are recognizably human, but they are not our sort (though they are infinitely more entertaining than that stuffy Victorian nemesis of Holmes). We watch them in the same way that Jimmy Cap of *Pronto*—himself one—studies bugs at Butterfly World.

Often the minor figures—the cops, record executives, bodyguards, parasites, and bimbo girlfriends—surprise us despite their small roles by being fully rounded and contributing to the true-to-life background of Leonard's busy canvasses. Their intrusive presence and their breezy chatter fill the spaces between those low-key, marginal guys we may have seen before and the ones we would approach only if they were behind steel bars or thick plate glass. Leonard's conviction that the right characters will tell their own stories may be critically naive, since both are products of his imagination, but his focus is sound. Characterization always takes precedence over plot in serious writing. To give characters an ambiguity and complexity absent in the flat figures of pop fiction, he has long relied on providing them changes of heart that caused an impatient reviewer of *Glitz* to say: "Bad-seeming characters turn out to be noble . . . many of the wise guys and enforcers are revealed as deeply OK."[7] A trifle overstated, this critical conclusion contains a grain of truth. In both Chili Palmer books, *Get Shorty* and *Be Cool*, callous stooges sweeten perceptibly as the stories unfold, so that Elliot Wilhelm (aka Willie Willis), described by Raji as "liking to hurt people," and the Bear (whom Chili has to grab once by the crotch and throw down a flight of stairs and once knee in the face) end up on the side of the angels. Thus Leonard risks being mechanical in attempting to avoid the predictable.

Themes

Similarly, Leonard's novels seek to transcend escapist fiction thematically. Although often his good characters end "happily and the bad unhappily," such is not invariably the case; nor is it ever intrusively so. In other words, Leonard does not identify theme with moral, or morality with didacticism. His major themes are very few. He always applauds self-reliance in its unsullied Emersonian form. A man must follow his conscience and confront adversity wherever he finds it. When three hoodlums approach Harry Mitchell in *52 Pick-Up* with a blackmail demand and later murder his girlfriend, Harry never hesitates to take them all on. Of course, since they are intellectually sluggish and emotionally undeveloped, he has a slight edge in the unequal combat. "Assholes" is one of the most derogatory terms in the Leonard vocabulary, and Harry's opponents are assholes to a man.

Self-reliance, initiative, and self-control are the qualities a man or woman must cultivate in life, though the last of these makes Leonard's love scenes more restrained and self-conscious than most in popular fiction. The heroes of these stories improvise marvelously. Faced with imminent violence from a six-foot-five, 260-pound "Samoan," Chili Palmer distracts the fellow by discussing opportunities for him in the movies, an attraction no Leonard character can ignore. When Vincent Mora wants to convince Ricky Catalina that he's an imported hit man, he borrows a paring knife from a bartender to use as a prop in a *Godfather*-like scenario he invents on the spot: "Do I cut your dick off and stick it in your mouth before I shoot you. . . . Or do I shoot you and then cut off your dick? . . . I'm not up on any of your quaint guinea customs" (*Glitz,* 132).

The idea of living by a code is so deeply ingrained in these books that it becomes in parody form the structure for the early novel *Swag (Ryan's Rules).* In it Jack Ryan composes 10 rules for success in armed robbery, the career he and Stick have chosen for themselves. Breaking their own rules—failing to be true to oneself—leads to their downfall. But Leonard's most sympathetic characters seldom betray their codes. They may falter in judgment or display a pardonable weakness, like taking three sexual partners in one night as Stick does in *Swag.* But Jack Foley *(Out of Sight)* never promised anyone—let alone himself—that he'd give up robbery. Slighting his responsibility to his ex-wife is another matter, however, and he feels understandably guilty about his treatment of Adele. More seriously, Harry Mitchell's infidelity to Barbara created the circumstances he's in. His reconciliation with this admirable woman in *52 Pick-Up* is seen as right, and as expiation for his lapse, since the betrayal of an honest mate—treacherous ones are another thing—cannot be confused with recreational sex or the erotic high jinks of the bachelor felons on the singles scene in *Swag.*

In his review of *Riding the Rap,* Scott Bradfield puts his finger on the theme that most frequently finds expression in these stories, asserting, "When you owe the dealer, you gotta pay."[8] In none of these novels is there a free lunch. Everyone pays full price, including women. Carolyn Wilder gets badly knocked about because she insists on playing the hotshot lawyer even if it means opposing good guys like Raymond Cruz and the Detroit police. Her setback is temporary, however, most likely because she is a woman (and they are more often victims than victimizers), but also because she is a workaholic, for Leonard displays a Calvinistic respect for labor.

The really rotten pay with their lives. Those who break the law but hurt only themselves, or others who richly deserve it, may escape if they're lucky. Sometimes you pay when you have done nothing wrong, like Bryan Hurd and Kathy Baker, or John Russell of *Hombre,* but most often the guy who does his job, whether making moonshine or making book, comes to a good end.

Point of View and Dialogue

Leonard tells his stories almost without exception from the omniscient point of view in the third person. Reasons for his choice can only be surmised. However, a third-person perspective, whether omniscient or limited omniscient, was the almost universal choice of Western pulp writers, and Leonard's Arizona stories are nearly all in the third person. On the other hand, detective stories from this period (as well as earlier and later on) are frequently first-person narrations. It is likely, then, that Leonard established what would become a lifelong habit in the fifties and grew so comfortable with that narrative perspective that he has never considered changing it.

Undoubtedly, the immediacy of the narration seemed less desirable in a genre attempting to project the aura of a bygone era. In suggesting a distant past and a remote area, the third person—with its potential for objectivity and lack of involvement—would appear a better choice to a less experienced writer. Its versatility and popularity must have been other factors that appealed to Leonard, who learned to use it fearlessly, unintimidated by its inherent risk of loss of coherence, as he grew adept at shifting from one character to another, even to those of minor significance, without losing the unity of his story. At his hand, the omniscient point of view becomes an asset in achieving proportion and perception.

Leonard's narrator is so unobtrusive that we are frequently unaware of his existence. Instead we seem not in his presence at all but rather in the mind of some character or another. *Out of Sight,* one of Leonard's most accomplished narrations, offers convincing illustration of his effortless mastery. The novel opens: "Foley had never seen a prison where you could walk right up to the fence without getting shot"(1). Because the narrator refers to the protagonist as "Foley," the passage might appear to be from a conventional third-person perspective; but by that standard, the "you" would qualify it as a second-person narration (a rare form, but not unknown, as Robert O'Connor's well-received *Buffalo Soldiers* [1993] testifies). Aside from the reference to Foley, the observation about the prison seems Foley's own. In fact, most of the narrator's remarks and observations might just as well be those of Foley: "He watched a shifty colored guy come out for a pass and get clotheslined going for the ball, cut down by another shifty colored guy on defense. The few white guys, bikers who had the nerve and the size, played in the line and used their fists on each other, every down. No Latins in the game" (*Out of Sight,* 2). Here the diction "colored," "clotheslined," "shifty," as well as the sentiment and final sentence fragment express Foley's thoughts so perfectly that the role of an intermediary appears superfluous.

The whole first chapter of *Out of Sight* belongs only to Foley, but the second one abandons him to introduce a new figure, Karen Sisco, who is treated as Foley was: that is, any line savoring of observation or judgment (as opposed to simply advancing the narration) seems as much hers as the narrator's. Thus the following sentences describing Karen's arrival at nightfall at a prison can be considered either as the narrator's statement or as Karen's observations: "Lights were coming on, spots mounted high that showed the compound with its walks and lawns; at night it didn't look all that bad. She lit a cigarette and dialed a number on her car phone," (*Out of Sight,* 15). The aesthetic judgment is certainly a shared one, and even the activities described ("she lit a cigarette and dialed a number") don't seem as much recorded acts as merely self-aware moments. The distance between narrator and character is all but imperceptible.

The brief third chapter of the novel does for Foley's pal Buddy what the first two did for Foley and Karen: three chapters, three new characters, all of whom come together in the fourth. Although Buddy's role in *Out of Sight* is small, Leonard accords him no less attention than the others when he's onstage. Entering into the minds of figures like Buddy gives Leonard the opportunity to write extended dialogue as a character recalls verbatim what he or others said at a specific time in the past. Leonard has grown so skillful at riveting dialogue that he uses it sometimes for pages at a time, and instead of merely relying on dialogue to advance the narration, he now employs it to replace conventional narration. For example, to apprise us of Foley's hapless criminal career and describe the kind of guy he is, Leonard has Buddy think back on his long association with his friend as he waits for him to emerge from a tunnel some convicts have dug for a jailbreak. Buddy recalls a telephone conversation with the incarcerated Foley, who had come to Florida to see his ex-wife and ended up in the slammer again:

> "Remember how she wrote the whole time we're at Lompoc?"
> "After she divorced you."
> "Well, I was never much of a husband. Never helped her out with expenses or paid alimony."
> "How could you, making twenty cents an hour?"
> "I know, but I felt I owed her something."
> "So you did a bank in Florida," Buddy said.
> "It reminded me of the time in Pasadena. I come out and the goddam car wouldn't start."
> "You talked about it for seven years," Buddy said, "wondering why you didn't leave the engine running. Don't tell me the same thing happened in Florida."
> "No, but it was like that."(*Out of Sight,* 24)

Leonard's highlighting of "ear-perfect whip smart dialogue" con-
tributes mightily to the success of his traditional third-person omniscient point of view.[9] Reveling in the present tense, making use of "goes"
for "says," and leaving out conjunctions like "if" or "when," it strikes a
contemporary note that is complemented by allusions to sports, music,
current events, movies, and TV shows and displays a sense of humor
funnier for the fact that his speakers haven't a clue they are funny.
Upstairs in the fleabag La Playa Hotel in *LaBrava,* two Cuban exiles are
conducting business:

> "Any pistol you want," Javier said, "wholesale price to a Marielito.
> Machine gun one-third off. MAC-10 cost you eight hundred."
> "Something small," Cundo Rey said.
> "You want a snubbie. This one, .38 Special, two-inch barrel. Same
> kind the Charlie's Angels use."
> "Yeah?"
> "Also Barney Miller."
> "Wrap it up," Cundo Rey said. (*LaBrava,* 136)

Leonard's effortless control of point of view, together with dazzling
dialogue, may not result in "high literature" (as Newgate Callendar
observes in his review of *Unknown Man # 89*), but it lifts Leonard's
brand of escapist literature to something not far from it.[10]

Serious versus Pop

Serious literature demands, among other things, an emotional response;
its perceptions and insights must be felt, not simply acceded to intellectually. No less a figure than Jonathan Edwards, seeking to promote the
Christian faith in eighteenth-century New England, had proclaimed
that it was not enough to comprehend religious doctrines but that they
must move the "affections" (i.e, the emotions). In attempting to provide
an emotional experience to his congregation, Edwards preached terrify-
ing sermons such as "Sinners in the Hands of an Angry God." Leonard
knows instinctively what Edwards meant. But he is not willing to take
the shortcuts of so much escapist literature and manipulate the feelings
of his readers. Escapist literature tends to rely excessively on responses to
the sentimental, the frightening, the romantic, and the comic. Poe
observed that "the death of . . . a beautiful woman is . . . the most
poetical topic in the world" because it has an emotional "effect" on the
reader.[11] Many Victorians—like Dickens—knew, however, that the

death of a child would bring the tears even faster. To be sure, Leonard allows the death of one beautiful woman in *Split Images,* but apart from such rare incidents, he skirts the sentimental. He never indulges in emotion for its own sake. His comic perception forbids it. His comedy is organic, growing out of his postlapsarian worldview that human behavior is almost always out of synch with the divine plan. As the level-headed Bill Hill of *Touch* puts it, baiting his hard-shell Baptist wife: "You know why Baptists never fuck standing up, Barbararose? They don't want God to think they're dancing" (90). Like Barbararose, most people are dummies, not so much living lives of quiet desperation as always noisily missing the point, getting their values ass backwards. Thus Leonard's humor—even jokes—promotes the defeat of the sentimental by being satiric.

No one, it is likely, ever read Leonard's thrillers for their love scenes, curiously low-key and chaste even when featuring bare bodies and a graphic detail or two. But romance plays a role in each one, and many will find that in books like *Rum Punch* and *Out of Sight,* his treatment of love possesses an undeniable charm.

Of course, Leonard does not hesitate to take full advantage of suspense, to cultivate it as each book hurries to "act 3." But here again he does not go in for cheap effects, the literary equivalent of yelling "boo" to scare someone in the dark. We earn our gooseflesh with *Freaky Deaky* or *Maximum Bob,* often having to put down the book either to prolong the effect or to regain our composure. But to criticize a thriller for scaring a reader is like complaining that a sonnet has 14 lines. Terror belongs to the nature of the genre. Legitimately, we may only judge how skillfully suspense is used or avoid crime stories entirely. Working inside constrictive limitations, Leonard does a bang-up job as he "pulls the old cards from his sleeves and shuffles them a new way" in every book.[12]

Because his novels are not whodunits, Leonard labors under no obligation to scatter clues about, to eliminate suspects, or to build suspense in a creaky variety of artificial ways. The scares proceed naturally from the situations, appearing more a part of real life than gimmicks slapped on. *Killshot,* with its stalked victim, may lack the scope and intensity of *Les Miserables* or *Crime and Punishment,* but like them, it generates a terror that uncovers and defines human nature rather than merely providing agreeable shudders.

In creating and maintaining suspense while avoiding the machinery used to accomplish that end, Leonard validates his reiterated claim that he avoids the expected while admitting that the expectations of commercial fiction serve as a guideline for his art. Not to fall over the edge requires that he is constantly aware that the edge is there.

Integrity

Although he tiptoes the line between serious and popular fiction with a success that startles reviewers, his enormous popularity suggests that he must be supplying an identifiable "need" or writing "formulaically," as if there were a recipe to guarantee the best-seller.

While there is certainly no such recipe (speculation on the ingredients of the best-seller being "about as reliable as astrology," as George Stevens wrote more than a half century ago), it is possible to identify certain characteristics, habits, and directions of popular fiction, many of which Leonard accepts, uses, and ignores as the case may be.[13] He never worries unduly about overproductivity or concerns himself about the changes to his novels demanded by movie producers or purchasers of his screenplays once they leave his hands. Nor does he apologize for his whopping income, indications to the purist that a writer's integrity might be questioned. To Leonard, however, integrity means the freedom to entertain while writing as well as he can according to his standards. He plans his books in three sections of equal length that he calls "acts" (90,000 words plus or minus), finding the first of these the easiest, and the second the hardest (because here any lapses of the first 140 or so pages of typescript come back to haunt him).

As a former writer of Westerns, he knows that "exotic" settings delight a mass audience, but the definition of that word has changed since Frank Luther Mott used it in his discussion of the best-seller in *Golden Multitudes*.[14] For the detective story, the city has long been exotic; and in our own time, various areas of the United States have enjoyed popularity in crime stories and have even become regarded as imaginative landscapes. Detroit and South Florida work for Leonard because they are familiar to him, but he has not been inextricably bound to either locale.

The Formulaic

Leonard's plots contain large doses of guns, action, and violence, as we have seen, certainly enough to satisfy escapist tastes. He introduces most characters in his "first act," where they interact and go on to become involved in a kidnapping or robbery in the "second act" before he untangles things in the third. Although he is extremely creative in the milieus he invents, taking the reader to smart Hollywood restaurants, the Havana of the Spanish-American War, or a rock concert, he relies on a number of familiar devices in one book after another: thus the appearance of the two women, the "caper," the psycho, and the shootouts. He favors exciting conclusions, *Dragnet*-style throwaway lines to end chapters or subsections, and multiple betrayals as well as a host of expendable contrivances like the house under siege, car chases, and contests to the death—none of which would raise an eyebrow in the mass market. In short, he actively seeks to entertain while remaining more interested in character than plot.

His characters are contemporary, though not people he knows firsthand. Rather, his blacks, Latinos, ex-cons, cocktail waitresses, and bail bondsmen are people he has read about in newspapers or been introduced to through contacts arranged through his research process. Still, they more than pass muster. Many are deliciously sleazy, but even when they drive a Rolls or a Mercedes, they are good enough to hold the reader's interest. That a number of them—not the psychos, naturally—change for the better in the course of a book may be regarded as part of Leonard's genial vision rather than a surrender to an enduring feature of popular fiction—the profound change of a character at a moment's notice.

Stylistically, writers of commercial fiction do not approve of innovation. They avoid experimentation because they seek to attract readers, not to make them think. The language of popular novels as well as the sentence structure and frequency of abstract words or ideas is determined by readability or governed by the same demand that directs the controlling premises of the plot. But Leonard doesn't worry overmuch. His rapid dialogues, borrowing from the movies, start in medias res. Scenes shift swiftly, another device he has gleaned from films, and often become shorter as he builds to a suspenseful climax. He is a careful writer, choosing the mot juste in both dialogue and narration. His diction is never careless, and his breezy dismissal of Fenimore Cooper's logorrhea suggests agreement with Hemingway's assertion that the classic American writers "did not use the words people have always used in speech," resulting in a usage in tune with so much good writing today.

Earlier, Leonard sometimes deliberately failed to identify a character for a page or two to encourage reader attention, but he has largely discontinued that practice. He will still begin a chapter or subsection without identifying a character, however, and he periodically records short conversations labeled with speaker's names in the form of a playlet. But this practice, meant to call attention to the dramatic nature of the utterances, could confuse no reader.

Timeliness or topicality is another matter often of advantage to the immediately popular book, and here Leonard is relentlessly au courant. His references to the cult of Elvis Presley, Bowl games, headline stories, movies, rock and roll, and current issues lend his stories an undeniably with-it air. Up-to-the-minute problems such as the aftermath of the Vietnam War, abuses of the probation system, Rust Belt agonies, women's issues, and the dilemmas of a multicultural society surface effortlessly. Rarely handled in slick or trendy fashion, they become genuine sticking points in these fast-moving dramas, and his nearly pharmacopoeial familiarity with the drug culture exudes a coplike authority.

Leonard is never preachy. He considers it pretentious to claim greater sensitivity to contemporary problems than other writers. While his celebrated humor draws on a mastery of the resources of language and rhetoric, it depends even more on a recognition of the incongruous than on maintaining a consistent satirical edge, something foreign to his genial outlook. He rejects the role of a reformer whose cityscapes imply criticism of social injustice. A commonsense approach to his material assists him in avoiding romantic excesses in what are essentially adventure tales, as well as in depicting his heroes, whose chiseled features are realistically softened by the Christian morality they—and he—espouse: decent, conventional, and acceptable. On the other hand, his picture of America as Y2K nears is harsh, if not bitter: a country of venal judges, decent cops, and recidivist convicts; a materialistic society where marriages regularly fail, faith has faltered, and colors and creeds are thrown willy-nilly together amid generous quantities of drugs, sex, and rock and roll.

An aura of honest bafflement about so much of modern life—the "gray area," to use a favorite Leonard expression picked up from a Detroit detective—complements the hope that decency, using one's head, courage, and loyalty will see one through. By no means infallible guarantees of success, they lead the good guys to happy endings some of the time, but as often to indeterminate ones.

Just as there is a thin line between the good and the bad, so is there between their goals, and Leonard spends a good deal of time sounding the ancient distinction between what is desired and what is desirable. The good guys (and gals) like dope, sex, and rock and roll, too. But they practice restraint, self-discipline, and moderation in their pursuit. They don't sip bourbon all day long like Dale Crowe Senior or hunt for teenage sexual partners like Chip Ganz. They reward themselves with a joint, a cold beer, consensual lovemaking, and a little Aerosmith.

Treading the Line

In conclusion, Leonard's books resemble popular or escapist fiction in respect mainly to his goal of winning an audience with a lively adventure story, his implicit assertion that a human being can always retain dignity, and his belief that the death of a hero must be avoided or at least shown not to be in vain. But they show important differences, too. He maintains considerable artistic autonomy. He refuses to provide readers with idealized depictions of characters with whom to identify. His voice is constantly liberal, tolerant, and fair-minded; he has no axes to grind or political or social agenda to advance. He avoids ephemeral issues while embracing topicality.[15] He emphasizes characterization at the expense of plot. But his plots do not write themselves, as even he acknowledges in less fanciful moments when, for example, he speaks of the need a story has for a "McGuffin." This term, borrowed from Alfred Hitchcock, refers to a device that generates events in a story (like the "caper") or a secret that must be revealed (like the origin of the alligator in *Maximum Bob*).

Leonard is content to expose in casual fashion such absurdities as the total failure of the American prison system without becoming a crank about it. (Indeed, where would Dutch Leonard be without his Angolas, Jacksons, or Lompocs?) His treatment of sex is forthright but neither graphic nor coy like the interminable affair arch-rival Robert B. Parker's sleuth Spenser conducts with the bluestocking Susan Silverman. Finally, Leonard's local color is so low-key, calling attention to itself so minimally, that Detroit and Miami seem only two more American cities, not atmospheric hot spots full of hard-breathing costumed extras.

Chapter Seven
The Movies

Of Leonard's 35 full-length books, not more than two or three have escaped movie options either for general distribution or TV. Of these, many have already appeared, but many also remain on tap. In addition, starting with *The Moonshine War,* he has written a number of original Hollywood screenplays, most of which have reached the screen. Although he sometimes dismisses the movies as a secondary interest, there merely to finance his novel writing, at other times he will admit to having film possibilities firmly in mind, so that his disclaimer must be taken with a grain of salt. In assessing Leonard's connection to the movies, we must remember several things: first, he is an avid moviegoer himself, often seeing several films a week and frequently viewing films at night at home on cable TV and on video; second, his long-time agent H. N. Swanson was primarily a Hollywood agent, and Swanie regarded all writing as fodder for celluloid; third, Leonard saw early in his career that movies could provide an income the pulps never could. "Three-Ten to Yuma" brought in $90 from *Dime Western* in 1953 in contrast to the $4,000 Hollywood paid for the story's film rights.

Working with movies from the days he wrote for the Encyclopaedia Britannica Films to the present moment, Leonard has acquired a professional knowledge of all aspects of the business, from screenplay writing to directing and the arcana of distribution and division of profits and losses. Both *Get Shorty* and *Be Cool* show an insider's knowledge of the making of movies and the politics involved in bringing them to the screen, and they, along with *Stick,* satirize the world of spoiled stars, schlock directors, and slippery financing as no novice could.

In the past, Leonard regularly borrowed ideas from movies, as, for example, almost every reviewer of *3:10 to Yuma* pointed out by invoking *High Noon;* and he still does, as the narrator of *Get Shorty* acknowledges when Chili Palmer disables the Bear in a Hollywood restaurant, grabbing him by the crotch and pitching him down the stairs: "There was a scene like it in an Eastwood picture."

The process is one of cross-fertilization. He gives and he takes. He as often visualizes a scene from a movie when writing a book as he imagines how something in a book will play on the screen. In his novels, he uses cinematic techniques that have become second nature after decades of moviegoing and screenwriting. In *Get Shorty* he includes whole pages from a script of *Mr. Lovejoy,* a movie Harry Zimm was trying to finance, and several characters in the novel discuss scenes and motivation as well as explain what abbreviated screenplay directions like "POV" (point of view) and "INT" (interior shot) mean. Commenting on Leonard's debt to film, George Grella perceptively notes that "he moves the angle of vision rapidly and frequently, for example, by cutting from character to character, point of view to point of view; the quick, smooth changes of scene, story, and people impart a Dickensian liveliness and daring to his novels, along with a paradoxically old-fashioned omniscience."[1]

As far as judging the movies made of Leonard's books and stories, there is perhaps no better critic than Leonard himself. At least he agrees more often than not with movie audiences and reviewers. Of Warner Brothers' *The Big Bounce* (1969) with Ryan O'Neal, sold to the studio for $50,000 by H. N. Swanson even before Fawcett Books bought the novel, Leonard says in agreement: "The woman in front of me said to her husband, 'This is the worst picture I've ever seen.' "[2] Almost as bad was *The Moonshine War* (MGM, 1970), made from Leonard's first Hollywood screenplay. Universally panned by puzzled critics unsure of whether the tedious story was meant as satire or drama, the movie, according to Leonard, suffered from poor direction and awful acting, especially Richard Widmark's portrayal of Emmet C. Taulbee, the dentist from hell.

In coming years, many more movies of Leonard books will play in theaters around the world, since large numbers of screenplays sit in various stages of unreadiness, being written or rewritten, considered for one star or rejected by another, or caught in the toils of studio politics. Each hot new book or film sends underlings scurrying to check the current status of Leonard properties to figure out what may be resuscitated and produced for profit using the formula that no money is really made until three times production costs are met.

Out of Sight, for example, was not the blockbuster that Universal needed in 1998, but neither did it go the disastrous route of several other productions of the financially shaky studio that year. Leonard's reaction is an insouciant shrug: Once the film rights contract is signed, it's out of his hands.

Early Films

The first two movies to be based on Leonard material, *3:10 to Yuma* and *The Tall T,* earned their author little money. Both began as pulp stories published in 1955. Leonard had nothing to do with either once it was sold, and both were augmented by other hands to bring them up to screen feature length.

Each is surprisingly good. In *3:10 to Yuma,* a properly humble man of the soil (Van Heflin) brings a cocky Glenn Ford to the train that will take the bandit to the territorial prison. The haunting title song sung by Frankie Laine, never as popular as that from *High Noon,* holds up as well as the movie itself and the brief, moving performance of Felicia Farr (Emmy), whose role was added. A "tainted" woman, she mourns the fate of the gallant bad man—and her own; she is a flower of remarkable beauty who wastes her sweetness on the desert air.

In Technicolor, *The Tall T* features Randolph Scott, the poor man's Gary Cooper, and villain Richard Boone, who reappears in *Hombre* a decade later. Proud that he avoids the predictable—"Never . . . did I stage a fast-draw shootout in the street"—Leonard facetiously called the scene where Randolph Scott blasts Skip Homeier under the chin with a shotgun, rather than indulging in the customary fistfight, "a defining Elmore Leonard moment."[3] But the violence and unpredictability contribute to a fine performance in this seldom-seen classic directed by Budd Boetticher, called by Jim Hitt "an extremely faithful adaptation that is even better than the good short story on which it is based."[4] The plot involves the efforts of Scott and Maureen O'Sullivan to turn several outlaws against one another—a favorite Leonard ploy—and the liberation of Loretta, who blossoms into womanhood under favorable circumstances.

Hombre (Twentieth Century Fox, 1967) starred the popular Paul Newman as the Mexican American John Russell, who had been kidnapped as a child and raised among the Apaches. Wearing a $450 black wig for the movie's early minutes, the blue-eyed Newman out-Apaches the Apaches in emotionless stoicism for large stretches of this epic of the Old West. *Hombre* borrows from *Stagecoach* (1939), as a motley group of frontier settlers—slightly more predictable than those of the novel—travel together across the stark Arizona landscape to Bisbee. Their coach is held up on the way by bandits in cahoots with one of the passengers, Cicero Grimes (Richard Boone), who is aware that Dr. Alexander Favor (Frederic March), an Indian agent from the San Carlos reservation, is carrying bundles of cash embezzled from the Apaches under his supervision. The bandits' failure to achieve their objective leaves everyone dependent on Russell, a man they despise, to guide them to safety.

Hombre is faithful to Leonard's story, a fast-paced, suspenseful tale in the tradition of Hollywood classics that show a disparate group interacting under extreme conditions. As in those earlier pictures, *Hombre* asserts the human need for mutual responsibility, reaffirming what Hemingway had reminded us of in the book Leonard kept by his side in those days, that "no man is an island."

Bristling with the distrust against white men of his adopted brothers, the Apaches, Russell proves not as icily remote as he first appeared and ultimately gives his life for the others when he exposes himself to danger to rescue Audra Favor (Barbara Rush). As the snobby young wife of the crooked agent, her role does not allow for much improvisation, and she is doubly handicapped by the black wig she wears, more awful even than Newman's.

Although the characters are largely stock types, their trials crossing the desert and the suspense of the chase command our interest right up to the gunfight at the end. *Hombre* stacks up as one of Hollywood's superior Westerns despite a degree of predictability and stretches of dialogue when characters such as Jessie (the whore with the heart of gold) announce ponderously: "We better deal with each other out of need and not merit." By and large, "the picture as a whole is well worth your attention—as is any film that succeeds in being entertaining while condemning intolerance and cupidity," as Philip T. Hartung put it in his *Commonweal* review.[5]

Valdez Is Coming (United Artists, 1971), filmed in Spain at the end of the Civil Rights era, features another noble man of color whose habit of long suffering ends when he turns his righteous indignation against Frank Tanner. Roberto Valdez (Burt Lancaster) is another blue-eyed Mexican suffering the racial injustices of white America. As a downtrodden sheriff allowed to arrest drunks only in the Mexican part of town, Lancaster shuffles and scrapes properly, but once he has decided to raise money for the Indian wife of a black former buffalo soldier he has inadvertently killed, a transformation takes place. Tugging on the form-fitting jodhpurs he once wore with the U.S. Cavalry and unpacking the well-oiled weapons he used fighting Apaches, the reborn Lancaster goes on a one-man crusade in behalf of the rainbow coalition. His earlier humiliation and a mock crucifixion he endures identify him—like John Russell—as a redeemer. *Valdez Is Coming* is undiluted Western as one good man takes on many bad ones, and the action and scenery are breathtaking. But Gay Erin's (Susan Clark) relation both to Valdez and Tanner is as problematic—read "clumsy"—as in the novel, and Lancaster's casting will seem to film buffs to be the big star's personal competition with Marlon Brando's Oscar-winning Zapata. Not quite in a league with *Hombre*, *Valdez* is still furlongs ahead of the average horse opera.

Other Westerns to reach the screen include *Last Stand at Saber River*, a Turner movie shown on TV in 1997 with Tom Selleck playing the lead. Based on the 1959 novel, it is a thoughtful but undistinguished account of a returning Confederate veteran seeking to put the war behind him with the help of his determined wife.

The earliest Leonard effort on TV was *Moment of Vengeance*, a *Saturday Evening Post* story appearing on Schlitz Playhouse on 2 October 1956. Angie Dickinson, a newcomer, played the daughter in a production *Daily Variety* damned with faint praise: "The offbeat twists of this psychological western [make] it an interesting effort although touches of hokum and a static overtalky quality combine to mar the total effect."[6]

The Border Shootout (Turner, 1989), loosely based on Leonard's second novel, *The Law at Randado*, attracted little attention and has just about slipped out of sight. Although the film contains a serviceable plot, an elderly Glenn Ford takes little interest in his role, huffing and puffing as he throws punches in a clumsy production with slow-motion shootouts à la Sam Peckinpah and musical motifs reminiscent of the spaghetti Westerns. The dialogue is packed with anachronisms, and the Indians are among the least convincing ever seen.

Leonard wrote several screenplays in the seventies after *Moonshine War*, among them *Joe Kidd*, made into a successful Clint Eastwood film, and *Mr. Majestyk*, written first as a brief outline with Eastwood in mind. When he declined, it was bought by the producer Walter Mirisch, who got Charles Bronson for the lead; and Leonard turned the completed script into a novel, reversing the usual procedure. The movie, about a melon grower with a checkered past who gets mixed up with an organized crime figure, is an action-adventure story with lots of car chases and crashes. Nancy Chavez (Linda Cristal) drives Vincent Majestyk's (Bronson) pickup like James Bond. The truck seems to spend as much time in the air as on the ground. Bronson's performance as a tough, do-it-my-way, uncompromisingly honest Western hero is more than usually wooden, and his opponent Frank Renda (Al Lettieri) chews the scenery shamelessly. Snarling and shoving his henchman about, Renda shows so little regard for the hired help that it's a wonder he can keep any. But instead it is Majestyk whose *braceros* have been intimidated by the bad guys into leaving him at harvest time. Steadfastly loyal Mexicans brutalized at night and houses under siege are familiar Leonard touches from earlier Westerns and mark this film as a transition on the way to crime fiction. *Mr. Majestyk* pops up frequently enough on TV to satisfy the legions of aging Bronson fans.

The Eighties

Not for 11 years after *Majestyk* would another Leonard novel be released by Hollywood: *Stick* (Universal, 1985), directed by and starring Burt Reynolds. On this movie, the usually mild-mannered Leonard grows hot under the collar. Paid $35,000 by Universal for rights and for a screenplay, Leonard was delighted when Roy Scheider agreed to take the leading role. But when Burt Reynolds offered to both direct and star in the picture, it was handed over to him: "Leonard was shown a preview of the movie, which was supposed to have been based on the screenplay he had written. At 6 A.M. the next morning he rose to compose a four-page letter to Reynolds detailing his objections, mainly about the direction of the film. Changes were subsequently made and some scenes reshot, delaying the film's release for several months. When it finally came out in the spring of 1985, the revised version was even worse" (Geherin, 96). The new and improved *Stick* bears little resemblance to Leonard's spare, sinewy work, and the Reynolds version is neither hip nor cool, just another heavy-handed action film with a cut-rate Ian Fleming conclusion.

In 1974 Leonard had sold the rights to *52 Pick-Up* to an Israeli film company that fundamentally altered the story, changing the setting from Detroit to Tel Aviv, and making the main character the American ambassador. This new rendition came out a decade later in the United States as *The Ambassador,* with Robert Mitchum and Rock Hudson in his last screen appearance. In 1986 the real *52 Pick-Up* opened in movie theaters; Leonard had overseen the screenplay, though he took little part in its actual writing. A violent, tough film that Judith Crist described as "nasty" and "gritty," *52 Pick-Up* has proved too strong fare for many who would agree with *Video Movie Guide* some years later that "mean and nasty" was a more fitting description. Coarse dialogue, nudity, and suggestive situations are arguably appropriate to the nature of the material, but the squeamish would do well to avoid several scenes of appalling brutality, especially the "snuffing" of a half-naked, terrified girl tied to a chair. Acting is first-rate in this thriller, moved from Detroit to Los Angeles, about a self-made industrialist (Roy Scheider) who single-handedly takes on a band of blackmailing pornographers who have abducted his wife by cleverly turning them against each other. Roy Scheider (as a husband repentant of his midlife affair with a peep-show model) and Ann Margaret (as his classy, forty-something wife) unite in a struggle of decent, flawed people against vermin. The movie is vintage Leonard.

Although he concedes limply that Jimmy Smits's job as Vincent Mora in *Glitz* "was okay," Leonard was not enthusiastic about that 1988 NBC Movie of the Week.[7] Nor was *Daily Variety,* which viewed the film (based on his first novel on the *New York Times* best-seller list) as being about as faithful to Leonard as a convict's wife.

To give Mora better motivation in solving her murder by Teddy Magyk (John Diehl), this version makes Iris Ruiz (Tasia Valenza), a Puerto Rican chippy (a semiprofessional prostitute), his erstwhile squeeze. In addition to this false move, the NBC movie embraces the old the-dumb-cops-have-it-all-wrong cliché as the Atlantic City police insist Iris's death was a suicide prompted by her failure to make it as a showgirl. Mora knows better.

Because *Glitz* was a network production, the language was expurgated, if not emasculated. The *Boston Globe* blamed scriptwriters Alan Trustman and Steve Zito for "wash[ing] the characters' mouths out with soap."[8] Although John Diehl came across more convincingly than Jimmy Smits ("as tough as Lassie's mom"), this movie pleased no one.[9]

Cat Chaser (Vestron Video, 1989), filmed mostly in Florida and Old San Juan, Puerto Rico, is a better-than-average crime flick and a much-better-than-average TV movie. Very slightly dumbed down, it contains steamy love scenes and de rigueur cable nudity—including the frontal male variety—that could be edited out if alternate rushes don't exist somewhere. A voice-over attempts to link three disparate plot strands: George Moran's (Peter Weller) sentimental journey back to the Dominican Republic, where his Marine platoon (Cat Chaser) took part in street fighting during the U.S. incursion; his romance with sexy Mary Delaney de Boya (Kelly McGillis); and the caper planned by Jiggs Scully (Charles Durning). This device works inconspicuously much of the time, though it occasionally grows portentous, as at the end when it announces after George has shot Scully: "He won't be George Moran again." Charles Durning's Jiggs Scully is provocatively menacing, an infinitely better job than his bewigged Chucky Gorman in *Stick*. Frederic Forrest, a veteran of many a TV feature, distinguishes himself in a production where the acting seldom rises much above adequate. *Cat Chaser* sticks pretty close to the novel, allowing for chunks of Leonard's surefire dialogue in a screenplay he coauthored. Carping viewers will ask questions like why General de Boya let George out of his house alive only to send his stooges after him the next day. But the movie's glitzy, fast pace generally eclipses such lacunae. *Cat Chaser* entertains, making no claims to anything else.

The Glorious Nineties

Get Shorty (MGM, 1995), with John Travolta, Gene Hackman, Rene Russo, and Danny DeVito, is Leonard's all-time favorite Leonard movie, "the best adaptation I've had," he says, and the one he finds most faithful to the Leonard "sound."[10] *Get Shorty,* with a script by Scott Frank, tells how a good-natured Florida loan shark (based on a guy who worked for Leonard's private eye classmate Bill Marshall) tried to get into the movie business. Reviews were great, and in its first week, the picture reached number one in America. Director Barry Sonnenfeld claimed that its success was due to Leonard's creating funny characters who don't know they're funny, but he had been doing that for years. Scott Frank declared he had "messed" as little as possible with the book's dialogue and merely tried to provide the story the structure sometimes slighted in the novels and their film adaptations. To accomplish this goal, he dumped a subplot and ended with the bumping off of the villain Bo Catlett. Leonard dismissed the changes, saying publicly: "It's different, sure, but Barry and Scott brought this to life. And I had a good time watching it."[11]

The nineties proved to be a golden decade for Leonard, with the colossal success of *Get Shorty* serving as an impetus for the filming of other novels, both early and late. Thus *Gold Coast,* published in 1980, showed up as a TV film in 1997. Written two years before *Cat Chaser,* the novel is one of those that profited by the success of *Get Shorty*. It shares with *Cat Chaser* a couple of situations: protagonists living in Florida who turn out to be both from Detroit; and Karen DiCilia being married to a wealthy, older tyrant who had problems with a country club back in Detroit. In fact, before passing away from a heart attack, Frank DiCilia hired Cal Maguire (David Caruso) to hold up the country club as punishment for rejecting his membership. Now he is trying to punish his wife from beyond the grave for suspected infidelity by seeing that she is denied male companionship after his demise. He has left behind orders that Dorado Management ensure that she establishes no relationships, a task that falls to Roland Crowe, one of those mean-as-a-snake good old boys in whom Leonard so delights. The movie revels in dazzling beachside estates and provides a neat inside view of a dolphin show. But the story is uneven and unconvincing, mainly because Karen starts out as a hometown girl in distress, impulsive and emotional, but ends as a calculating bitch goddess out of a noir film (a preview of Jeanie Breen in *LaBrava*), coolly drilling Roland Crowe in the last reel without a second thought.

Despite minor setbacks, such as the failure of *Split Images* ever to be released, or the dispute with Dustin Hoffman over *LaBrava* that sent the screenplay back to rewrites (where it still remains), triumphant years like 1997 redeemed them when in addition to *Gold Coast, Touch* (United Artists), *Pronto* (Showtime), and *Jackie Brown* (Miramax) hit movie and TV screens. A low-budget film, *Touch,* released in selected locations, made production costs, paid salaries, and firmed acting reputations for Bridget Fonda, Christopher Walken, Skeet Ulrich, and comedian Tom Arnold. *Time* recognized that "*Touch* was never meant to be *Get Shorty*. . . . rather a wintry meditation on the difficulties of sustaining authentic faith in the age of tele-morality."[12]

Pronto comes close to *Jackie Brown* (opening half a year later) as a diverting action film with a well-done love story. Taking a slight bow to that old Clint Eastwood movie *Coogan's Bluff,* a cowboy-hatted U.S. marshal (James Legros) puts a saucer-eyed Italian hit man back in his box—permanently—amid the colorful background of South Beach and Rapallo, Italy (actually filmed on the Greek island of Corfu). Director Jim McBride shoots an intelligent film, once focusing the camera on a woman's well-turned hindquarters in tight jeans to suggest lust, but later showing Harry Arno's (Peter Falk) shuffling bare feet to suggest the impotence of age. McBride also manages to deal nicely with a major problem in the book, the sympathy the crotchety Harry fails to generate for himself. Instead *Pronto* becomes a story of the passing of the old order and the arrival of the new. Like Lear or Ibsen's Masterbuilder, Harry does not want to retire gracefully from his active life as a bookie, though he talks endlessly about doing just that after the Super Bowl.

Forced to flee the Mob by running to Italy, he takes along with him for entertainment tapes of his day-to-day betting transactions. In a gentle final scene, after his girl has left him for a much younger Raylan Givens, we see that losing her doesn't mean much to the mulish old egotist after all.

Some reviewers objected that the wonderful Glenne Headley turns to Raylan, since measured by celluloid standards, at age 38, she was seen as being too old. After the last credits have faded from the screen, others might ask why that bug-eyed thug let Raylan go free when he once had him at his mercy, or what would have happened in the penultimate scene, the dining-room shootout, if the room hadn't been empty. But *Pronto,* good as it is, is not for all time.

With a Christmas Day release and a $15 million price tag, Quentin Tarantino's *Jackie Brown* was eagerly awaited by movie buffs and Hollywood hucksters alike, both of whom had visions of another *Pulp Fiction* (1994) in their heads. That film, shot for $8 million, had taken in $213 million and won universal praise, and though Tarantino had not been able to do it again, here was another chance.

He changed Leonard's Jackie Burke in *Rum Punch* to Jackie Brown, an African American played by Pam Grier, best remembered for her roles in blaxploitation films of the 1970s including *Blacula* (1972), *Foxy Brown* (1974), and *Sheba* (1975). The plot stayed the same minus neo-Nazis, jackboys, and Max Cherry's conniving wife. Jackie Brown, a savvy flight attendant for a small Mexican airline, crosses gunrunner Ordell Robbie (Samuel L. Jackson), who works his illegal activities with the dubious aid of an ex-con (Robert De Niro). Rediscovered like Grier was veteran actor Robert Forster as Max Cherry, the bail bondsman responsible for coping with the bad guys and conducting a moving romance with Grier.

Big stars like Robert De Niro and Michael Keaton in small roles, rather than the other way around, give *Jackie Brown* a touch of—if not class—understated extravagance. Tarantino has a way of burning his bridges, going for broke in style. For example, this film probably uses the word "nigger" more than any other in the history of cinematography—always, however, from the mouth of a black. It's violent, profane, and pop, and gives the Delfonics and the Supremes more play than a seventies Motown radio station.

The kudos earned by *Jackie Brown* shine forth in critic Roger Ebert's review: "It is a film of subtle and engaging gifts, which lurk beneath the surface of its crimes, scams, murders, drugs and colorful Tarantinian dialogue. It will entertain his fans, but it will also reward thoughtful analysis: It is a more revolutionary film than it appears,"[13] Ebert goes on to praise what others have so often remarked on: the dialogue, of course, "unexpected scenes," and plenty of provocative characters: "We keep meeting more people—their friends, lovers, hangers-on, confidants." As a film critic, Ebert is dazzled by "the texture of the pacing and dialogue" of Leonard's books, qualities that translate beautifully to the screen.[14]

Expectations fanned by the success of *Jackie Brown* and the recent memory of profits garnered by *Get Shorty* prompted troubled Universal to pay Leonard $3 million outright for *Out of Sight* (1998). It would be directed by Steven Soderbergh, whose career mirrored Tarantino's. Soderbergh had had a series of flops with the artistic films he made after opening eyes in 1989 with *Sex, Lies, and Videotape,* which took top prize at the Cannes Film Festival when he was only 26 years old.

Unfortunately for the film studio, *Out of Sight* did little to improve Universal's balance sheet for the year. Expected to be a bombshell, it has proved more a bomb, having (at the time of this writing) brought in only about $40 million, making the film in Hollywood's eyes little more than a break-even picture.

George Clooney, the long-lashed heartthrob of TV's *ER,* plays Jack Foley, and relative newcomer Jennifer Lopez is Karen Sisco, a federal marshal. Early in the movie, we witness Foley's Florida prison breakout and escape ride in a car trunk with Sisco, one of a half-dozen drolly moving scenes in the book featuring "the sort of self-assured, sexually charged banter we've rarely heard since the heyday of Cary Grant."[15] Foley is a gentlemanly bank robber who avoids guns and has had a good deal of bad luck. The focus of the film is a big robbery at the house of a white-collar crook whom the boys met in the joint. This ends in a shootout during a nocturnal blizzard in a wintry Detroit suburb. But the heart of the movie beats to a different rhythm, the premise that if Foley and Sisco had met under different circumstances—not in the trunk of a getaway car during a jailbreak—who knows what might have happened. Each thinks this could be the one.

Times critic Janet Maslin joined (or led) the chorus of voices praising *Out of Sight*'s screenplay "adapted with deftness and fidelity by Scott Frank [*Get Shorty*] who knows exactly how to translate Mr. Leonard's narrative voice to the screen."[16] She liked the ending, too, which produced a cameo surprise and a big, fat ray of hope for Jack Foley that is absent in the novel. If only critics bought movie tickets, *Out of Sight* would have had a different history.

Somewhat later in the summer of 1998, several pilot episodes of *Maximum Bob* appeared on ABC at 10 P.M. eastern standard time. Although Beau Bridges did a good job as the testy Florida judge, the broad humor and zany comic episodes had little to do with Leonard's book, and as the ratings came in, hopes for a regular series in the fall faded before the geraniums did.

Notes and References

Chapter One

All page references to Leonard's works are to the editions cited in the endnotes and not necessarily the editions that are listed in the bibliography.

1. Marguerite Harper to Elmore Leonard, 20 November 1951, uncataloged Leonard correspondence, Elmore Leonard Collection, University of Detroit Archives.

2. David Lehman, "Playing for Keeps," *Newsweek,* 4 February 1985, 80.

3. Scott Bradfield, *Times Literary Supplement,* 21 July 1995, 21; Bill Ott, *Booklist,* March 1995.

4. David Geherin, *Elmore Leonard* (New York: Continuum, 1989), 136; hereafter cited in text.

5. Readers will recall that Virgil Webster in *Cuba Libre* has an elaborate tattoo with flowers, a gravestone, and a cross, lettered "In Memory of Mother," not because his mother died but because he just liked the motif. Also Walter Majestyk, a justice of the peace in *The Big Bounce,* has been given Leonard's service duty at the airstrip on Los Negros in the Admiralty Islands, as well as the scam that Leonard and others carried out, selling Navy and Air Force personnel cheap souvenirs—bracelets and jewelry they made adorned with stones traded from the natives. Walter Majestyk has no connection to Vince Majestyk in *Mr. Majestyk* (1974); Leonard just liked the name.

6. Raymond Chandler, *Trouble Is My Business* (New York: Ballantine Books, 1972), 3.

7. Leonard, "One Horizontal," (unpublished story), Elmore Leonard Collection, University of Detroit Archives.

8. Gregg Sutter, "Elmore's Legs," interview by Alec Wilkinson, *New Yorker,* 30 September 1996, 45.

9. Elmore Leonard, *Pronto* (New York: Dell, 1995), 13; hereafter cited in text.

10. Apparently both of these stories were sold by literary agent H. N. Swanson, who would also sell *Hombre* but lost track of Leonard among his galaxy of writers until he was sent *Mother, This Is Frank Ryan* in 1966.

11. Three more, since in most respects *Cuba Libre* (1998) is as much a Western as *Valdez Is Coming* (1970) and *Forty Lashes Less One* (1972).

12. Leonard, *Get Shorty* (New York: Dell, 1991), 359.

13.   Charles Heckleman to Elmore Leonard, 17 November 1967, uncataloged Leonard correspondence, Elmore Leonard Collection, University of Detroit Archives.

14.   H. N. Swanson to Elmore Leonard, 25 September 1968.

15.   Elmore Leonard, *52 Pick-Up* (New York: Avon, 1983), 108.

16.   Leonard, *Swag* (New York: Dell, 1984), 173.

17.   Gregg Sutter, "Getting It Right," *Armchair Detective* (Winter 1986): 6. Sutter mentions professor Benjamin Hellinger.

18.   Ben Yagoda, "Elmore Leonard's Rogues' Gallery," *New York Times Magazine,* 30 December 1984, 26.

19.   Gregg Sutter, "Dutch," *Detroit Monthly,* 1980, 54.

20.   Peter S. Prescott, *Newsweek,* 14 November 1983, 114.

21.   Christopher Lehmann-Haupt, *New York Times,* 7 October 1983, 25.

22.   Herbert Mitgang, *New York Times,* 29 October 1983, 17. Leonard found Mitgang's recognition of him amusing, since he felt he had been doing pretty well up to this point.

23.   Leonard regards it as an accident that *Glitz* achieved his breakthrough, believing that either *Stick* or *LaBrava* might have achieved the same distinction. In readership and critical recognition, "my time had come," he says.

24.   Gregg Sutter, "Advance Man," *Armchair Detective* (Spring 1986): 163.

25.   Stephen King, "What Went Down When Magyk Went Up," *New York Times Book Review,* 10 February 1985, 7.

26.   Leonard's sales put him in the middle ranks of popular American writers.

27.   Robert Worth, "Plumbing the Shallows," *Commonweal* 5, no. 122 (August 1995): 24.

28.   Elmore Leonard, *Out of Sight* (New York: Delacorte, 1996), 16; hereafter cited in text.

Chapter Two

1.   Director Quentin Tarantino saw no problem in changing Jackie Burke to a black woman (played by Pam Grier) and focusing attention on her rather than Ordell Robbie in *Jackie Brown,* Tarantino's film version of *Rum Punch.*

2.   Elmore Leonard, *Escape from Five Shadows* (New York: Dell, 1994), 60.

3.   Lawrence Grobel, "Pulp Fiction," *Playboy,* May 1995, 140.

4.   Leonard, *The Bounty Hunters* (Boston: Houghton Mifflin, 1953), 4; hereafter cited in text.

5.   Leonard, *Bandits* (New York: Warner Books, 1988), 119.

6.   Gregg Sutter writes not quite accurately: "He got most of his sound and images out of three books: *The Truth about Geronimo, Adam's Western Words,*

and *The Look of the Old West*. The rest he pulled out of stories in the old *Arizona Highways*." In "Getting It Right: Researching Elmore Leonard's Novels, Part 1," *Armchair Detective* (Winter 1968): 7.

7. John C. Cremony, *Life among the Apaches*, with an introduction by Robert B. McCoy and John T. Strachan (Glorietta, N. Mex.: Rio Grande Press, 1969), 79; hereafter cited in text.

8. Leonard is somewhat vague about his firsthand knowledge of Cooper. However, he enthusiastically approved of Twentieth Century Fox's 1992 version of *The Last of the Mohicans*, especially praising the performance of Madeleine Stowe.

9. Leonard, *Last Stand at Saber River* (New York: Bantam, 1988), 1; hereafter cited in text as *Last Stand*.

10. Elmore Leonard, introduction to *Hombre* (New York: Armchair Detective Library, 1989), n.p.; hereafter cited in text.

11. Leonard, *Valdez Is Coming* (New York: Dell, 1993), 150; hereafter cited in text as *Valdez*.

12. Leonard, *Gunsights* (Thorndike, Maine: Thorndike Press, 1979), 283; hereafter cited in text.

13. Reporters appear in several Westerns, and Leonard is thoroughly aware of the role they—including Stephen Crane—played in the Spanish-American War. They also figure prominently in *Cuba Libre*. However, he denies he had in mind Vietnam, where reporting, especially on TV, exposed so much of the dishonesty of the campaign that in time the public came to regard the war as foolish and wrong rather than noble and just.

Chapter Three

1. Michael Wood, "Down These Meaner Streets," *Times Literary Supplement*, no. 4366 (5 December 1986): 1370.

2. Elmore Leonard, *The Big Bounce* (New York: Mysterious Press, 1986), 148; hereafter cited in text.

3. The original title of the book, *Mother, This Is Jack Ryan*, is meant to reflect the delight Nancy expected to take at her socialite mother's discomposure when her daughter introduced a former migrant worker and ex-convict as a prospective husband.

4. Leonard, *52 Pick-Up* (New York: Avon, 1983), 42; hereafter cited in text.

5. Jack Ryan appeared in *The Big Bounce*, where he mentioned that he used to break into houses with a black man named Leon Woody. In *Swag*, Frank Ryan says once: "Well, years ago I was into a little burglary, B. and E. Me and another guy, we didn't do too bad. But then he went into numbers or something—he was a black guy" (Leonard, *Swag* [New York: Dell, 1984], 11; hereafter cited in text). Although a black character named Leon Woody appears in *Swag*, Frank does not seem to know him. Finally, Jack Ryan in *Unknown Man*

 # 89 is clearly the same Jack Ryan of *The Big Bounce.* There does not seem to be any special significance to any of this, except that Leonard responds to certain names, names he feels fit his characters and stimulate his imagination.

Leonard has flirted several times with using a continuing character, aware of how successful they have been in the market he occupies. But the notion is antithetical to his proclivity for tiring of a figure, or for his need to change one. He sees the demand to produce a consistent, regularly appearing character as a restriction that he does not want to assume. At the same time, he chafes at any limitation forbidding him to resurrect or to mention a previous character.

6. Newgate Callendar, "Criminals at Large," *New York Times Book Review,* 4 April 1977, 34.

7. Leonard, *Unknown Man # 89* (New York: Avon, 1984), 125; hereafter cited in text as *Unknown.*

8. Someone must have clarified the issue for him, however, since in *The Switch* Richard Edgar Monk, a militant neo-Nazi, explains the difference to Ordell Robbie and Louis Gara: "Here's your famous Walther P38, some people think it's a Luger" (Leonard, *The Switch* [New York: Dell, 1990], 40; hereafter cited in text).

9. In *The Switch,* Ordell Robbie recalls Bobby Lear's murder, but Leonard is now calling the hotel the Montclair.

10. The movie *Ruthless People* (1986), with Danny DeVito and Bette Midler, put the kibosh on production plans for a film of *The Switch* with Diane Keaton in the leading role, since it too concerned a kidnapped wife whom a husband had no desire to ransom.

11. Leonard, *City Primeval* (New York: Avon, 1982), 118, 119; hereafter cited in text as *City.*

12. Leonard is on shaky ground here. The chance that the make and model of the pistol could be established by examining the lead slugs recovered at the scene of either the first or second crime is extremely unlikely. The police never examine the gun itself, a model manufactured in huge numbers for the German military and exhibiting no particularly distinctive marks.

13. James Russell Lowell, "A Fable for Critics," in *Major Writers of America,* ed. Perry Miller (New York: Harcourt, Brace and World, 1962), 830.

14. Leonard, *Freaky Deaky* (New York: Warner Books, 1989), 335; hereafter cited in text as *Freaky.*

15. A favorite Leonard term. He used it to describe John Gotti in an interview with me, 8 June 1997.

16. Leonard, *Killshot* (New York: Warner Books, 1990), 280; hereafter cited in text.

Chapter Four

1. *New York Time,* 26 July 1998, 16. Michigan is high for the Midwest (average 6.5), and Florida low for the South (average 9.0).

2. Elmore Leonard, *Gold Coast* (New York: Dell, 1990), 218; hereafter cited in text.

3. Because Karen would have been born in 1936, it is unlikely that she would have identified much with Virginia Hill, whose prominence in America would have come when Karen was 14 years old. This is another instance of Leonard taking earlier events, movies, strikes, and attitudes and bringing them forward in time.

4. Leonard, *Split Images* (New York: Avon, 1983), 51; hereafter cited in text as *Split*.

5. Leonard, *Cat Chaser* (New York: Avon, 1983), 279; hereafter cited in text as *Cat*.

6. John Leonard, *New York Times,* 11 June 1982, 29.

7. Jonathan Yardley, "Elmore Leonard: Making Crime Pay in Miami," *Washington Post,* 20 February 1983, 3.

8. Leonard, *Stick* (New York: Avon, 1984), 52; hereafter cited in text.

9. George Stade, "Villains Have the Fun," *New York Times Book Review,* 6 March 1983, 41.

10. Leonard, *LaBrava* (New York: Avon, 1984), 24; hereafter cited in text.

11. LaBrava admits that he saw one Jean Shaw film when he was 12 years old. As a child, he seems to have been a bit precocious in being attracted to women more than 20 years older than he.

12. References to height are frequent in Leonard's books. Harry Arno in *Pronto* tells Joyce, "He was the height of the average U.S. fighting man in World War Two, five nine" (*Pronto,* 5). Lawrence Grobel's profile in *Playboy* (May 1995) opens: "Master crime writer Elmore Leonard is shrinking. He used to be 5'9", he says, but not anymore."

13. Leonard, *Maximum Bob* (New York: Dell, 1992), 5; hereafter cited in text as *Bob*.

14. *Elmore Leonard's Criminal Records*, BBC Television, 1991.

15. Leonard, *Rum Punch* (New York: Dell, 1993), 292; hereafter cited in text.

16. Leonard, *Riding the Rap* (New York: Dell, 1996), 12; hereafter cited in text as *Riding*.

17. Leonard, "Trouble at Rindo's Station," *Argosy*, October 1953.

18. Leonard, "Trouble at Rindo's Station," in *The Tonto Woman* (New York: Delta, 1998), 320.

Chapter Five

1. Elmore Leonard, *Touch* (New York: Avon, 1988), 40; hereafter cited in text.

2. Leonard, *Bandits* (New York: Warner Books, 1988), 11; hereafter cited in text.

3. Leonard asked columnist George Will to compose the letter, but Will said that Leonard had gotten Reagan down better than he could. Leonard, interview by the author, 19 September 1998.

4. Although neither *Tobacco Road* nor *God's Little Acre* contains references to distilling whiskey, popular impression was that they did. The frontispiece blurb to the Signet Classic edition of *God's Little Acre* begins inaccurately: "Making plenty of love and liquor."

5. Leonard, *Get Shorty* (New York: Dell, 1991), 79; hereafter cited in text.

6. Leonard, *Glitz* (New York: Arbor House, 1985), 36; hereafter cited in text.

7. Leonard, *The Hunted* (New York: Mysterious Press, 1988), 136; hereafter cited in text.

8. Nestor Soto's henchman Avilanosa tells Eddie Moke: "Try to see if you can . . . not lose your pistols again."

9. Clancy Sigal, "Which Are the Bad Guys," *Listener* 117, no. 3006 (9 April 1987): 28.

10. Adam Begley, "Family Values for the Criminal Element," *New York Observer,* 8 May 1996.

11. Lawrence Grobel, "Pulp Fiction," *Playboy,* May 1995, 124.

12. Nicholas Chistopher, quoted in Michiko Kakutani, "Somewhere in the Night," *New York Times,* 28 March 1997.

Chapter Six

1. Patrick Meanor, "Introduction," in *Dictionary of Literary Biography,* vol. 130 (Detroit: Gale Research, 1993), xi.

2. Peter S. Prescott, *Newsweek,* 14 November 1983, 114; Christopher Lehmann-Haupt, *New York Times,* 7 October 1983, 25.

3. David Lehman, *Newsweek,* 4 February 1985, 80.

4. Elmore Leonard, *Out of Sight* (New York: Delacorte, 1996), 296; hereafter cited in text.

5. Robert Worth, *Commonweal* 122 (18 August 1995): 24.

6. Leonard, *Be Cool* (New York: Delacorte, 1999), 4; hereafter cited in text.

7. Luc Sante, *New York Review of Books,* 28 March 1985, 18.

8. Scott Bradfield, *Times Literary Supplement* 4816 (21 July 1995): 21.

9. Michael Kernan, quoted in "Elmore Leonard," *Contemporary Literary Criticism* 71 (1992): 206.

10. Newgate Callendar, *New York Times Book Review,* 22 May 1977, 33.

11. Edgar Allan Poe, "The Philosophy of Composition," in *The Viking Portable Library: Poe,* ed. Philip Van Doren Stern (New York: Penguin Books, 1945), 557.

12. Ralph Lombreglia, *New York Times Book Review,* 8 September 1996, 8.

13. Stevens entitled his book *Lincoln's Doctor's Dog* because he found from a study of best-sellers that readers showed interest in Lincoln, doctors, and dogs.

14. Frank Luther Mott, *Golden Multitudes* (New York, 1960), 290.

15. In *Bandits,* Leonard uncharacteristically condemns the American involvement in Nicaragua going on at the time.

Chapter Seven

1. George Grella, "Film in Fiction: The Real and the Reel in Elmore Leonard," in *The Detective in American Fiction, Film, and Television,* ed. Jerome H. Delamater and Ruth Prigozy, Contributions to the Study of Popular Culture, no. 63 (Westport, Conn.: Greenwood Press, 1998), 37. Grella's essay, demonstrating how closely connected Leonard's books are to the movies—and how life imitates art—is totally convincing, though Grella tends to see Leonard as a talented movie buff rather than the initiate he actually is.

2. Lawrence Grobel, "Pulp Fiction," *Playboy,* May 1995, 124.

3. Elmore Leonard, "Get Dutch," interview by Patrick McGilligan, *Film Comment* 34, no. 2 (March–April 1998): 45.

4. Jim Hitt, *The American West from Fiction (1823–1976) into Film (1909–1986)* (Jefferson, N.C.: McFarland, 1990), 233.

5. Philip T. Hartung, "Black and White and Red All Over," *Commonweal* 86, no. 5 (April 1967): 152.

6. "Schlitz Playhouse," in *The Variety Television Reviews, 1946–1956,* vol. 1, 2 October 1956 (New York: Garland Publishing, 1989).

7. Lawrence Grobel, "Get Elmore," *TV Guide,* 1 August 1998, 24.

8. Richard Dyer, "TV Notes," *Boston Globe,* 21 October 1988, 44.

9. Ibid.

10. Bernard Weinraub, "Getting *Get Shorty* off the Page to the Screen," *New York Times,* 25 October 1995, C19.

11. Ibid.

12. Richard Schickel, "Jesus Christ, Superdude," *Time,* 24 February 1997, 67.

13. Roger Ebert, "*Jackie Brown* Confirms Quentin Tarantino Is the Real Thing," *Marin Independent Journal,* 4 January 1998, D4. In this same review, Tarantino says, "Probably the number one thing I'm proudest of is that 50 percent of the dialogue . . . is mine and 50 percent of it is Dutch's, and I think it's seamless. I think you really can't tell."

14. Ibid.

15. Robert W. Butler, "*Out of Sight* Lives Up to Its Title," *Kansas City Star,* 28 June 1998, 5.

16. Janet Maslin, "He's a Thief, She's a Marshal, They're an Item," *New York Times,* 26 June 1998, E14.

Selected Bibliography

Primary Works

Novels

The Bounty Hunters. Boston: Houghton Mifflin, 1953.
The Law at Randado. Boston: Houghton Mifflin, 1954.
Escape from Five Shadows. Boston: Houghton Mifflin, 1956.
Last Stand at Saber River. New York: Dell, 1959.
Hombre. New York: Ballantine, 1961.
The Big Bounce. New York: Fawcett, 1969.
The Moonshine War. New York: Doubleday, 1969.
Valdez Is Coming. New York: Fawcett, 1970.
Forty Lashes Less One. New York: Bantam, 1972.
Mr. Majestyk. New York: Dell, 1974.
52 Pick-Up. New York: Delacorte, 1974.
Swag. New York: Delacorte, 1976.
The Hunted. New York: Dell, 1977.
Unknown Man # 89. New York: Delacorte, 1977.
The Switch. New York: Bantam, 1978.
Gunsights. New York: Bantam, 1979.
City Primeval. New York: Arbor House, 1980.
Gold Coast. New York: Bantam, 1980.
Split Images. New York: Arbor House, 1981.
Cat Chaser. New York: Arbor House, 1982.
Stick. New York: Arbor House, 1983.
LaBrava. New York: Arbor House, 1983.
Glitz. New York: Arbor House, 1985.
Bandits. New York: Arbor House, 1987.
Touch. New York: Arbor House, 1987.
Freaky Deaky. New York: Arbor House/William Morrow, 1988.
Killshot. New York: Arbor House/William Morrow, 1989.
Get Shorty. New York: Delacorte, 1990.
Maximum Bob. New York: Delacorte, 1991.
Rum Punch. New York: Delacorte, 1992
Pronto. New York: Delacorte, 1993.
Riding the Rap. New York: Delacorte, 1995.
Out of Sight. New York: Delacorte, 1996.

154

Cuba Libre. New York: Delacorte, 1998.
Be Cool. New York: Delacorte, 1999.

Short Stories

"Trail of the Apache." *Argosy,* December 1951.
"Apache Medicine." *Dime Western,* May 1952.
"You Never See Apaches . . ." *Dime Western,* September 1952.
"Red Hell Hits Canyon Diablo!" *Ten Story Western Magazine,* October 1952.
"The Colonel's Lady." *Zane Grey's Western,* November 1952.
"Cavalry Boots." *Zane Grey's Western,* December 1952.
"Law of the Hunted Ones." *Western Story Magazine,* December 1952.
"Under the Friar's Ledge." *Dime Western,* January 1953.
"The Rustlers." *Zane Grey's Western,* February 1953.
"Three-Ten to Yuma." *Dime Western,* March 1953.
"The Big Hunt." *Western Story Magazine,* April 1953.
"Long Night." *Zane Grey's Western,* May 1953.
"The Boy Who Smiled." *Gunsmoke,* June 1953.
"The Hard Way." *Zane Grey's Western,* August 1953.
"The Last Shot." *Fifteen Western Tales,* September 1953.
"Blood Money." *Western Story Magazine,* October 1953.
"Trouble at Rindo's Station." *Argosy,* October 1953.
"Saint with a Six-Gun." *Argosy,* October 1954.
"The Captives." *Argosy,* February 1955.
"No Man's Guns." *Western Story Roundup,* August 1955.
"The Rancher's Lady." *Western Magazine,* September 1955.
"Jugged." *Western Magazine,* December 1955.
"Moment of Vengeance." *Saturday Evening Post,* 21 April 1956.
"Man with the Iron Arm." *Complete Western Book,* September 1956.
"The Longest Day of His Life." *Western Novel and Short Stories,* October 1956.
"The Nagual." *Two-Gun Western,* November 1956.
"The Kid." *Western Short Stories,* December 1956.
"Bullring at Blisston." *Short Stories Magazine,* August 1959.
"Only Good Ones." in *Western Roundup,* ed. Nelson Nye. New York: Macmillan, 1961.
"The Tonto Woman." in *Roundup,* ed. Stephen Overholser. Garden City, N.Y.: Doubleday, 1982.
" 'Hurrah for Capt. Early.' " in *New Trails: Twenty-Three Original Stories from Western Writers of America,* ed. John Jakes and Martin H. Greenberg. New York: Doubleday, 1994.

Story Collections

The Tonto Woman and Other Western Stories. New York: Delacorte, 1998. Reprints 18 early Western short stories and one new one, " 'Hurrah for Capt. Early' " (1994).

Anthologies

Dutch Treat. New York: Arbor House, 1985. Includes *City Primeval, The Moonshine War, Gold Coast*.
Double Dutch Treat. New York: Arbor House, 1986. Includes *The Hunted, Swag, Mr. Majestyk*.

Screenplays

The Moonshine War. MGM, 1970.
Joe Kidd. Universal, 1972.
Mr. Majestyk. United Artists, 1974.
High Noon, Part 2: The Return of Will Kane. CES, 1980.
Stick. Universal, 1985.
52 Pick-Up. Cannon, 1986.
The Rosary Murders. Take One Productions, 1987.
Desperado. Universal, 1987.

Miscellaneous

"Impressions of Murder." *Detroit News Sunday Magazine,* 12 November 1978.
The Courage to Change: Personal Conversations about Alcohol with Dennis Wholey. New York: Warner Books, 1986, 87–94.
"The Odyssey." Chapter 12 of *Naked Came the Manatee,* a novel with chapters by 13 Florida crime writers. New York: Putnam's Sons, 1995.

Interviews

I have ignored most of the dozens of Leonard interviews, since they are extremely repetitive.
Taped conversations with James E. Devlin, 19–23 June 1997 and 17–19 September 1998.

Secondary Sources

Complete Books

Geherin, David. *Elmore Leonard*. New York: Continuum, 1989. Insightful, thorough, and helpful.

Articles and Reviews

Current Biography Yearbook 1985, 264–68. New York: H. W. Wilson, 1985. Reliable quick reference through *Glitz*.
Grella, George. "Film in Fiction: The Real and the Reel in Elmore Leonard." In *The Detective in American Fiction, Film, and Television*, ed. Jerome H. Dela-

mater and Ruth Prigozy, 35–44. Westport, Conn.: Greenwood Press, 1998. Shows how Leonard has movies in mind when he writes.

Grobel, Lawrence. "Pulp Fiction." *Playboy,* May 1995, 122–24, 140–43. Generic Leonard interview on the eve of *Riding the Rap.*

Hynes, Joseph. " 'High Noon in Detroit': Elmore Leonard's Career." *Journal of Popular Culture* 25, no. 3 (Winter 1991): 181–87. Remarkably similar reading—but coincidental—to this volume on Leonard's worldview.

McGilligan, Patrick. "Get Dutch." *Film Comment* 34, no. 2 (March–April 1998): 43–53. Leonard talks shop on the movies.

Mitgang, Herbert. "Novelist Discovered after Twenty-Three Books." *New York Times,* 29 October 1983, 17. Leonard's "discovery" announced.

Prescott, Peter S. "Making a Killing." *Newsweek,* 22 April 1985, 62–67. Puts Leonard and *Glitz* in a sleuth's hall of fame.

Reed, J. D. "A Dickens from Detroit." *Time,* 28 May 1984, 84–86. Calls Leonard the "Dickens from Detroit" and lauds his "Panasonic ear."

Sutter, Gregg. "Dutch," *Monthly Detroit,* August 1980, 54–58.

———. "Getting It Right: Researching Elmore Leonard's Novels, Part 1." *Armchair Detective* (Winter 1986): 4–19. Appreciative treatment of a number of novels and accounts of how Leonard gets his details right by his researcher.

———. "Advance Man: Researching Elmore Leonard's Novels, Part 2." *Armchair Detective* (Spring 1986): 160–72.

Wilkinson, Alec. "Elmore's Legs." *New Yorker,* 30 September 1996, 43–47. Sketch of Gregg Sutter, Leonard's legman, with inside information on Leonard's work habits and methods.

Other Works Consulted

Adams, Ramon F. *Western Words: A Dictionary of the American West.* Norman: University of Oklahoma Press, 1968.

Bissell, Richard. *A Stretch on the River.* Boston: Little, Brown, 1950.

Brown, Jay A. *Rating the Movies for Home, Video, TV, and Cable.* Lincolnwood, Ill.: Publications International, 1990.

Cremony, John C. *Life among the Apaches.* Glorieta, N.Mex.: Rio Grande Press, 1969.

Davis, Britton. *The Truth about Geronimo.* New Haven, Conn.: Yale University Press, 1963.

Foster-Harris, William, and Evelyn Curro. *The Look of the Old West.* New York: Viking Press, 1955.

Freidel, Frank. *The Splendid Little War.* Boston: Little, Brown, 1958.

Hemingway, Ernest. *For Whom the Bell Tolls.* New York: Charles Scribner's Sons, 1940.

Hitt, Jim. *The American West from Fiction (1823–1976) into Film (1909–1986).* Jefferson, N.C.: McFarland, 1990.

Lockwood, Frank C. *The Apache Indians*. Lincoln: University of Nebraska Press, 1987.

Martin, Mick, and Marsha Porter. *Video Movie Guide 1992*. New York: Ballantine Books, 1991.

Parish, James Robert, and Michael R. Pitts. *The Great Western Pictures*. Metuchen, N.J.: Scarecrow Press, 1976.

————. *The Great Detective Pictures*. Metuchen, N.J.: Scarecrow Press, 1990.

Perrine, Laurence, and Thomas R. Arp. *Literature: Structure, Sound, and Sense*. 6th ed. New York: Harcourt, Brace, Jovanovich, 1993.

Stevens, George. *Lincoln's Doctor's Dog*. New York: Lippincott, 1939.

Swanson, H. N. *Sprinkled with Ruby Dust*. New York: Warner Books, 1989.

Utley, Robert M. *A Clash of Cultures*. Washington, D.C.: National Park Service, 1977.

Index

The Author

In his fourth decade at the College at Oneonta (State University of New York), where he is professor of English, James E. Devlin is the author of an earlier Twayne volume, *Erskine Caldwell*. By birth a Bostonian, he is, like Leonard, a product of a Jesuit College (Boston College) and a veteran. His advanced degrees are from Harvard and Binghamton University (State University of New York). A Fulbrighter in Goettingen, Germany, in 1976, he has written on German subjects from Heinrich Boell to Marlene Dietrich and in American literature on figures from Washington Irving and Hawthorne to Andre Dubus and Elmore Leonard. Since 1995 he has been coordinator of the biannual International James Fenimore Cooper Conference, held in Otsego County, New York, in July.

The Editor

Frank Day is a professor of English and head of the English Department at Clemson University. He is the author of *Sir William Empson: An Annotated Bibliography* (1984) and *Arthur Koestler: A Guide to Research* (1985). He was a Fulbright lecturer in American literature in Romania (1980–1981) and in Bangladesh (1986–1987).